SEASONS of the
CHRISTIAN LIFE

SEASONS of the
CHRISTIAN LIFE

Robert Cummings Neville

CASCADE *Books* • Eugene, Oregon

SEASONS OF THE CHRISTIAN LIFE

Copyright © 2016 Robert Cummings Neville. All rights reserved. Except for brief quotations in critical publications or reviews, no part of this book may be reproduced in any manner without prior written permission from the publisher. Write: Permissions, Wipf and Stock Publishers, 199 W. 8th Ave., Suite 3, Eugene, OR 97401.

Cascade Books
An Imprint of Wipf and Stock Publishers
199 W. 8th Ave., Suite 3
Eugene, OR 97401

www.wipfandstock.com

PAPERBACK ISBN 13: 978-1-4982-8618-3
HARDCOVER ISBN 13: 978-1-4982-8620-6
EBOOK ISBN 13: 978-1-4982-8619-0

Cataloguing-in-Publication data:

Name: Neville, Robert C.

Title: Seasons of the Christian life / Robert Cummings Neville.

Description: Eugene, OR: Cascade Books, 2016.

Identifiers: ISBN: 978-1-4982-8618-3 (paperback) | ISBN: 978-1-4982-8620-6 (hardback) | ISBN: 978-1-4982-8619-0 (ebook)

Subjects: LCSH: Sermons—American—21st century. | Methodist Church—Sermons. | Boston University—Marsh Chapel. | Title.

Classification: BV4254.2 N48 2016 (print) | BV4254.2 (ebook)

Manufactured in the U.S.A.   06/28/16

All Scripture quotations unless noted otherwise are taken from the New Revised Standard Version of the Bible, copyright, 1989, Division of Christian Education of the National Council of the Churches of Christ in the United States of America. Used by permission. All rights reserved.

For the Actual and Virtual Congregations of Marsh Chapel 2004–2005

Contents

Preface | ix

1. Sins: Nailed to the Cross | 1
   Psalm 85; Colossians 2:1–15 (11–19); Luke 11:1–13

2. The Potter's Vessels | 6
   Jeremiah 18:1–11; Philemon 1–21; Luke 14:21–33

3. The Value of Something Lost | 11
   Jeremiah 4:11–12, 21–28; Psalm 14, 1 Timothy 1:11–17; Luke 15:1–10

4. Living in Our Own Time | 17
   Jeremiah 32:1–3a, 1–15; 2 Samuel 11:27b—12:9; Luke 16:11–31

5. Religion for Reward | 22
   Lamentations 1:1–6; 2 Timothy 1:1–4; Luke 17:1–10

6. A New Covenant | 26
   Jeremiah 31:21–34; 2 Timothy 3:11—4:5; Luke 18:1–8

7. Humility and Exaltation: The Twenty First Sunday after Pentecost | 31
   Joel 2:21–32; 2 Timothy 4:1–8, 11–18; Luke 18:1–14

8. Conversion | 36
   Habakkuk 1:1–4; 2:1–4; 2 Thessalonians 1:1–4, 11–12; Luke 19:1–10

9. The Heavens, the Earth, the Sea, and the Dry Land | 41
   Haggai 1:15b—2:9; Psalm 145; 2 Thessalonians 2:1–5, 11–17; Luke 20:21–38

10. Endurance | 46
    Isaiah 65:11–25; 2 Thessalonians 3:1–13; Luke 21:1–19

11 To Be Awake | 52
    Isaiah 2:1–5; Romans 13:11–14; Matthew 24:36–44

12 Repent | 57
    Isaiah 11:1–10; Romans 15:1–13; Matthew 3:1–12

13 Inauspicious Beginnings | 62
    Isaiah 63:1–9; Hebrews 2:11–18; Matthew 2:11–23

14 Testimony to the Light | 68
    Isaiah 60:1–6; Ephesians 3:1–12; Matthew 2:1–12

15 The Name of Jesus: Baptism of the Lord | 73
    Isaiah 42:1–9; Acts 10:31–43; Matthew 3:11–17

16 Light, Vocation, Healing | 79
    Isaiah 9:1–3; 1 Corinthians 1:11–18; Matthew 4:11–23

17 To Know What Counts | 84
    Micah 6:1–8; 1 Corinthians 1:11–31; Matthew 5:1–12

18 Coping with Transfiguration | 89
    Exodus 24:11–18; 2 Peter 1:11–21; Matthew 17:1–9

19 Ash Wednesday | 94
    Joel 2:12, 11–17; 2 Corinthians 5:20b—6:10; Matthew 6: 1–6, 11–21

20 Temptation | 97
    Genesis 2:11–17; 3:1–7; Romans 5:11–19; Matthew 4:1–11

21 The Difference Faith Makes | 103
    Genesis 12:1–4a; Romans 4:1–5, 11–17; John 3:17

22 Seeing beyond Expectations | 108
    1 Samuel 16:1–13; Ephesians 5:1–14; John 9:1–41

23 Spirit and Flesh | 113
    Ezekiel 37:1–14; Romans 8:1–11; John 11: 1–45

24 The Power of Humility | 118
    Isaiah 50:1–9a; Philippians 2:1–11; Matthew 27:11–54

25 Teaching | 123
    Isaiah 50:1–91; Philippians 2:1–11; Matthew 21:1–11

26 "Father, into your hands I commend my spirit." | 128

27 Raised with Christ in Newness of Life | 131
    Romans 6:1–11; Matthew 28:1–10

28 The Day of Resurrection | 136
    Acts 10:31–43; Colossians 3:1–4; John 20:1–18

29 Meeting the Risen Christ | 141
Acts 2:14a, 31–41; 1 Peter 1:11–23; Luke 24:11–35

30 To Follow the Shepherd | 146
Acts 2:41–47; 1 Peter 2:19–25; John 10:1–10

31 "I Am the Way, the Truth, and the Life" | 151
Acts 7:51–60; 1 Peter 2:1–10; John 14:1–14

32 Forms of Love | 157
Acts 17:21–31; 1 Peter 3:11–22; John 14:11–21

33 Freedom of the Spirit | 162
Acts 2:1–21; 1 Corinthians 12:3b–13; John 7:31–39

34 Something New and Lasting | 167
Psalm 149; Song of Solomon 8:1–7

35 The Ambivalence of Family, or The Lesson of Hagar | 171
Genesis 21:1–21; Romans 6:1b–11; Matthew 10:21–39

Preface

The seasons of the Christian life are of many kinds. The round of the liturgical year is obviously one. I am a lectionary preacher and so follow the liturgical seasons closely; the sermons in this book are chronological and pick up in the summer of Lectionary Year C and move to Year A with Advent in the fall. Sermons for Advent, Christmas, Epiphany, the Transfiguration, Lent, Palm Sunday, Holy Tuesday, Good Friday, the Easter Vigil, Easter, and Pentecost are to be found here, each addressing its respective liturgical theme explicitly. But I am also a preacher in Marsh Chapel at Boston University, and at the time of these sermons, from July 2004 through June 2005, was Dean of Marsh Chapel and the University Chaplain. Unless otherwise noted, the sermons were preached at Marsh Chapel. So my work is oriented around the seasons of the academic calendar. The sermons here begin with a summer baptism homily and then move into welcoming students and their families in September, homecoming later in the fall, and so forth. Since all preaching is contextual, I should say that the academic year of these sermons also began with the baseball season in which the Boston Red Sox broke the Bambino's curse, defeated the Yankees for the American League pennant in four straight games after being three games down, and went on to win the World Series for the first time since Methuselah took his children to watch from the bleachers.

Perhaps the most significant sense of "season" in these sermons, however, is the political. These sermons, in chronological order here, began in the fall before the 2004 presidential election in which George W. Bush defeated Boston's favorite son, John Kerry. More than just a local favorite, Mr. Kerry represented the liberal aspirations of a great many citizens of Massachusetts, the bluest of the blue states according to most accounts. Many people in Boston saw the election as a test of American morality, one that we failed. After the election, when some pollsters had claimed that 80

Preface

percent of the American people who regularly attend church or synagogue voted for Mr. Bush, several of my congregants came to me to ask whether they should stop coming to church. Did Christianity really mean acquiescing in the militaristic, arrogant, greedy, and mendacious posture they attributed to Mr. Bush? Did the evangelical Right define Christianity?

I resolved then that my preaching had to intensify the effort to articulate a kind of Christianity other than that offered by the evangelical Right with which Mr. Bush had identified himself. My aim has been not only to articulate a Christianity of humility, peacemaking, and the cultivation of gentle souls, but to do so in increasingly explicit opposition to the preaching from the Right.

To do so was not at all emotionally congenial, for I am a liberal of the sort who lives out tolerance and wants to embrace everyone claiming to be a Christian within the Christian fold. I have spent many years in the United Methodist Church working to defuse tensions between Right and Left, especially within institutions of theological education. Although many preachers from the Right have had no compunction speaking out in forceful terms against more liberal Christianity on issues of personal and social morality, desirable patterns of the Christian life, and fundamental theological issues, preachers from the Left have been reluctant to reciprocate. Hence, we seem to have no position of our own, no claim to Christian history and authority. At the University, outside the School of Theology and the Chapel, people generally identify Christianity to me with Mr. Bush's evangelicalism. The same thing is true of people I meet in community groups, in casual meetings while traveling, even at the gym where everyone knows me as "the Reverend." This has not changed during the last decade.

Who is to say that a different vision of Christianity exists, one with a richer heritage and less connection with the defense of a particular narrow culture? Who is to say that Christianity really stands for what it alleges—love, peace, justice, and all those wimpy virtues preached in the Beatitudes—in the face of the public presentation of the evangelical Right, which so often is hatred of what it takes to be impure, war against what it takes to be evil, and the justification of defending what we have because we deserve it? I understand that this is not the way the saints on the evangelical Right think of themselves, but it is how they are seen from the liberal perspective that contextualizes their politics. The personal answer to my question is, that it is up to liberal colleagues and me to preach this alternative vision of Christianity with sharp articulation.

Preface

Although I have come strongly to believe that the conservative theology of the evangelical Right is destructive of the Christian life and that the way forward with the gospel in our time is through the development of a more liberal, ecumenical, and multicultural tradition, I say upfront that the conservative approach has a biblical warrant. If one looks, say, at the book of Daniel, the authentic letters of Paul (excluding Ephesians, Colossians, and the Pastorals), and the Book of Revelation, it is possible to see the background framing of Christianity to be a narrative account of a war between God and the devil, between the forces of good and those of evil. Both Jewish and Christian apocalypticisms of the centuries before and after Christ were influenced by the Persian dualism between good and evil divinities. Some statements attributed to Jesus in the Gospels can be read into this narrative frame. The emphasis on narrative as the primary form of Christian understanding has been powerful in the last century due to the influence of Karl Barth. The amazing popularity of the Left Behind series of books, a representation of classical narrative dispensationalism (to use the fancy theological jargon) illustrates the appeal of narrative, indeed, battle-narrative thinking. Politicians appeal to this battle-narrative version of Christianity when they rail against "evil empires" and nations constituting an "axis of evil." When the hugely criminal bombings of 9/11 called for a response, which should have been an international police action to root out organized terrorism, the Christian Right responded instead to calls to "war" because of its commitment to the battle narrative of us against evil. Terrorists, of course, just duck and move elsewhere when war machines come their way. So our government had to find some countries instead against which to make war. The Taliban government of Afghanistan rather approved of 9/11, although it did not fund or execute the tragic bombings. The Iraqi government of Saddam Hussein was not the best of the Middle Eastern dictatorships, but it seems to have had no connection with the 9/11 terrorists despite the attempt of our government to claim so after its other justifications for attacking and occupying Iraq collapsed. If you think you are in a war, then you have to find somebody to war against. That is, among other mistakes, a theological one.

An alternative reading of the Christian life, and of the Bible, is to subsume narrative elements within a larger background of the complex relationship between human beings and God. The wisdom literature of the Bible, such as Job, Ecclesiastes, Proverbs, Jonah, and most of the Psalms; the teachings of Jesus in the Gospels through parables and sermons; the books

Preface

of Ephesians, Colossians, and James, are about this complex and sometimes problematic relationship. The legal material in Exodus, Leviticus, Numbers, Deuteronomy, Ezra, and Nehemiah lays out patterns for how people, or at least Jews, are to live before God. The historical materials in Genesis, Exodus, Joshua, Judges, Ruth, and the books of Samuel, Kings, Chronicles, and Acts all read most plainly as stories of a people's developing relationship to God, not as incidents in a cosmic battle between God and Satan. The prophets, too, are primarily concerned about fidelity and infidelity in the relation between God and Israel, particularly in matters of justice, and what these things mean for Israel's fortunes in history; even the apocalyptic passages in Isaiah 21–27 pit God's consuming destruction against human misdeeds, not cosmic satanic forces. Although there are many narratives in this material, the narratives are mainly about people and their relations with God and one another, not about a cosmic drama. Liberal theologians, who read the Bible and the Christian setting as a matter of the relationship between God and human beings, thus emphasize the virtues of relationship, primarily love, justice, peace, mercy, forgiveness, humility, and other wimpy character traits. These traits look wimpy, of course, only to those who think virtuosity in the Christian life is booting backsides for Jesus.

Both conservative evangelical and more liberal preachers read the same Bible, of course, and play different though related roles in the same large and sprawling Christian movement. Preachers of the Right know about the Sermon on the Mount but embed it in the battle narrative in which Christ will come again to claim his own and stomp out the opposition. Preachers of the Left know about the apocalyptic imagery, especially in the New Testament, but construe that as literary intensifications of matters more directly described as elements of the relationship between God and people. Theologians who think of God primarily in terms of a cosmic battle narrative with evil necessarily construe God as finite in order to play roles in the narrative. Theologians who think of God primarily as the Creator in relation to human creatures accept the arguments of philosophical theologians from the earliest times that God is infinite. All finite things are created, and the Creator is not finite. This means, however, that all our references to God are symbolic, rarely if ever literally true. Good theology, and hence good preaching, knows how to use symbols without drawing the wrong inferences. For instance, we can call God the rock of our salvation without inferring that the proper study of God is geology. What are the limits of calling God Lord or King, suggesting a political relationship?

Preface

Imagining God in a cosmic battle with evil might have symbolic value in certain carefully circumscribed contexts, as does thinking of God in other anthropomorphic ways. Yet good preaching needs to clue people in to the limits of their symbols, and the conditions for their appropriate use. Most of these sermons deal explicitly with issues of how to read the Bible and understand basic Christian symbols. The theory of theological interpretation embodied in them, and sometimes explained directly, is clearly an alternative to the interpretation theories commonly employed by the religious Right (in Christianity, Judaism, and Islam).[1]

Three relational themes weave throughout these sermons that I would like to be seen as distinct, but that I fear will be read in a confused way.

First, I want to relate to my colleagues on the evangelical Right with respect and love, and with appreciation of our common heritage of the Bible and Christian historical traditions, sometimes with common denominational membership. With these colleagues, our disagreements come from different interpretations of the Bible, those Christian traditions, and our contemporary situation. There is no single interpretation within the Right or the Left.

Second, I want to relate to the political and cultural situation of the period of these sermons with criticism: criticism of the neocon philosophy, of the readiness to undertake preventative wars, of hypocritical justifications for war, and of economic and social policies that serve the rich at the expense of the poor. These criticisms are not new, and have their roots in the Bible. But they can seem to be attacks on the Christian evangelical Right because the government and social forces that are the targets of the attacks often justify themselves on evangelical grounds, and often are supported by evangelical Christians. It is confusing to separate love and respect for very conservative Christians from straightforward criticism of political and social policies with which they are frequently associated. I am sorry about that.

---

1. Readers who want an explanation of my interpretation theory in a full treatise can consult Robert Cummings Neville, *Truth of Broken Symbols*, SUNY Series in Religious Studies (Albany: State University of New York Press, 1996); those who want a full theological illustration of the theory should look at Neville, *Symbols of Jesus: A Christology of Symbolic Engagement* (Cambridge: Cambridge University Press, 2001). The systematic theological background for all this, set in the context of world religions, not only Christianity, is to be found in my trilogy: Neville, *Ultimates*, Philosophical Theology 1 (Albany: State University of New York Press, 2013); Neville, *Existence*, Philosophical Theology 2 (Albany: State University of New York Press, 2014); and *Religion* Philosophical Theology 3 (Albany: State University of New York Press, 2015).

Preface

Third, I want to promote in these sermons a liberal approach to Christian spirituality and morality. This is intended as a positive articulation of a Christian direction that is often missed because so many people think of Christianity only in terms of its Right, not its Left. So, here I have emphasized the biblical, especially the New Testament, symbols for liberal theology. More than most preachers, I emphasize interpretation of the biblical texts, and take seriously the discipline of the lectionary to deal with the hard texts, around the liturgical cycle. Although the strictly political arguments are often the same as would be given by Jewish, Muslim, or secular liberals, here I want to articulate the contours for a liberal Christian identity.

Some years ago I published a book of sermons titled *The God Who Beckons: Theology in the Form of Sermons*.[2] The subtitle is important. Sermons do have theological content, and it is my desire here to articulate a theology that offers an alternative to the public theology of so much Christianity these days. The sermons themselves, of course, make their own claims to represent the history, authority, and current cutting edge of Christianity. The sermons in the present book follow up on those in *Preaching the Gospel without Easy Answers*, preached the year before at Marsh Chapel, and I have to say that the sermons here do not present easy answers either.[3] But then, the questions are not easy, and they are very important. Why publish or read sermons a decade after they were preached? The lectionary gives them perennial significance. Their dates give them a living context.

Boston, Massachusetts
January 2016

---

2. Neville, *The God Who Beckons: Theology in the Form of Sermons* (Nashville: Abingdon, 1999).

3. Neville, *Preaching the Gospel without Easy Answers* (Nashville: Abingdon, 2005).

I

Sins: Nailed to the Cross[1]

Psalm 85; Colossians 2:1–15 (11–19); Luke 11:1–13

Last Sunday's sermon was about a very difficult text in Colossians whose point was that the death of Christ Jesus on the cross means that human beings, individually and in our communities, are reconciled to God.[2] The early Christians symbolized this in the imagery of animal and human sacrifice. I apologize for the complexity and far-fetched imagery in that text, and in my sermon. If your eyes glazed over for a bit last week, that is perfectly understandable. A preacher has the duty to deal with the hard texts and you might be comforted to know that I do my duty only rarely.

The texts for today from Colossians and also from Luke follow up on those from last week and are not difficult at all, you will be pleased to know. They have extreme and unusual imagery, but the point is brilliantly clear. Although life has many obstacles and problems, the only thing of ultimate importance that holds us back is our sin. But Jesus Christ has taken away our sin and we are free. Free! Free! And therefore we should ask the most of life, live it to the fullest, and rejoice that because we are related to Jesus the fullness of God is all around us.

---

1. Preached July 25, 2004, the eighth Sunday after Pentecost; the sermon hymn was "It Is Well with My Soul," with words by Horatio G. Spafford and music by Philip P. Bliss.

2. That sermon, "Christ the Image of the Invisible God," is number 2 in *Preaching the Gospel without Easy Answers*, 1–14. For those interested, the contrast between the two sermons might be interesting; it was interesting for the congregation.

Today's text from Colossians begins by enjoining us to live with devoted thanksgiving in the Christian faith. It warns us not to be taken captive by the deceitful philosophies of the pagan religions devoted to what the author calls "the elemental spirits of the universe." In the first century people believed that the universe was populated not only by the different kinds of angels I mentioned last week, the "thrones, dominions, rulers, and powers," but also by many other kinds of spiritual forces, some of which are demonic. The early Christians interpreted the pagan religions to worship one or more of these forces, and rejected all such paganism in favor of the worship of the High God, the Creator of everything in the universe including invisible spirits, the God of Abraham, Isaac, and Jacob, who was revealed in Christ.

We twenty-first-century people who worship in a university church are not likely to be tempted by first-century paganism, although we should not forget that many of our sisters and brothers in other lands do live very much in a world they see to be populated by spirits of all sorts. Our own brand of false worship is more likely to be devoted to what contemporary cynics say are elemental spirits.

The cynics among us say that power is our greatest desire, however we try hypocritically to be humble, so go after power honestly and ruthlessly. The cynics among us say that political dominance is the real goal of international politics, however we try hypocritically to represent ourselves as peacemakers, so go after dominance honestly and with all the might at our disposal. The cynics among us say that greed is the real underlying motive of all action, however we try hypocritically to represent ourselves as generous, so go after all we can get by any means we can get away with. These and other elemental forces in human society can become objects of worship, and the cynical people say to be honest about that. The Christian gospel says, No. Like the spirits created by God according to the first-century belief, power, political strength, and enjoyment of possessions are good things in their places, even necessary; but they cannot be worshiped without displacing worship of the true God. Give them up, says Colossians, and don't be deceived by the cynical philosophies.

Of course, giving up worship of such idols of our age is not easy. Part of the meaning of original sin is that we are committed to them and to the social structures that they rule, whether we consciously want to be or not. But Hallelujah! We are freed from bondage to sin. As Colossians put it in a striking metaphor, we are spiritually circumcised with Christ and have put on his spiritual flesh. Circumcision, you know, was the symbolic rite given to Abraham and his descendants that made them God's people and the heirs of God's promise to make them flourish. Spiritual circumcision makes us God's people and heirs to God's promise to bring us close. Spiritual circumcision means that all of us, Gentiles and Jews, are God's people. Christians carry the flesh of Christ on their bones.

Then Colossians has an even more powerful image. It says that Jesus's baptism was like his dying. To go down into the water is to die. When we Christians are baptized, as young Naomi Fassil will be this morning, this is like dying to our sins. We lose the flesh of sin. When Jesus rose up out of the baptismal water, this was like his rising from the dead. And so with us: when we rise from baptism we are already resurrected from sin and living with God. This is a different theology of baptism from that which says it is a bath that cleanses us from sins. It is more than being just an initiation rite into the Christian community. Rather, Colossians says that baptism is the rite of death and resurrection. The third chapter goes on to say that we, or at least the Christians in Colossae, have already died, spiritually, and are already raised with Christ in heaven. We are also living here in history, even while we "have been raised with Christ," and therefore we should "set our minds on things that are above." We should get our act together, put to death the practice of earthly evils. Colossians says,

> But now you must get rid of all such things—anger, wrath, malice, slander, and abusive language from your mouth. Do not lie to one another, seeing that you have stripped off the old self with its practices and have clothed yourselves with the new self, which is being renewed in knowledge according to the image of its creator. In that renewal there is no longer Greek and Jew, circumcised and uncircumcised, barbarian, Scythian, slave and free; but Christ is all and in all! (Colossians 3:1–11)

Baptism gives us a whole new self, and we have to learn how to live with that self in holy ways. What about the sins of our old self? They are "nailed to the cross"! We still have all the problems of life, of course, and we will sin in the future; but we are enjoying our true identity in heaven already, right now; we do not stumble on those problems because of our sins. They are nailed to the cross. Our old, sinful habits of addiction to power, dominance, greed, deceit, and countless other things might still be strong, but they do not control us, because our sins are nailed to the cross. Colossians tells us that in baptism we have already undergone death, and with that our sins and their due punishment are nailed to the cross. We have already undergone resurrection with Christ, and so we should live as already-resurrected people. What strange and yet powerful good news!

This theology of salvation is different from Saint Paul's, which says that we struggle through this life until we are saved at the end of it in a future resurrection when Jesus comes again. The problem with Paul's theology of salvation is that Jesus did not come soon as he expected, and despite Paul's claim that we have grace to live new lives now, he is easily interpreted to mean that present life is just a holding action until some future time. Paul's phrase is that we are "walking between the times." Justification by faith alone, one of Paul's famous doctrines, has been interpreted to mean that if we just believe, God will take care of us later. Colossians' theology says that we are already raised and live in the presence of God with Christ, and that life on earth is the very important task of sanctification, living in holy ways. Sanctification, for Colossians, is not earning salvation: we already have salvation in the baptismal form of death to our sins and resurrection to new life. Sanctification is the perfection of how to live in this world as holy people. The injustices of this world are a hundred times more horrific to us now, because we see them as infections of a world that should be sanctified. Addressing them cannot be put off until some future salvation. The Letter to the Ephesians and the Gospel and Letters of John agree with Colossians, as does the Methodist tradition on which this university and its chapel are based.

How should we live as holy people, already enjoying God's salvation and learning to live worthy of it in our daily lives? How should we live the life of renewal of the new self? Luke's version of the Lord's Prayer quotes Jesus saying that we should pray regularly to God as the hallowed or holy one whose holiness we approach. We should pray that earthly life be made like God's perfect kingdom. From this comes our commitment to justice. We should pray for continued forgiveness of sins we might commit as we too forgive those who sin against us. We should pray that we not fall into special trials or temptations, as these shall surely arise in daily life. Moreover, Jesus goes on to say, in Luke's account, that we should demand of the world the resources to be generous, like the man who pounded on his neighbor's door to borrow bread to entertain his visitors. Be persistent, said Jesus, in working for the resources to be generous. "Ask, and it will be given you; search, and you will find; knock, and the door will be opened for you.

For everyone who asks receives, and everyone who searches finds, and for everyone who knocks, the door will be opened."

Of course this does not happen every time, as the Crucified One came to know from personal experience. Sometimes our parents, or our communities, do give us snakes instead of fish, scorpions instead of eggs. But by and large God is generous, and we should look for grace in abundance as resurrected members of God's household. According to Luke, Jesus did not say that God will give us fish and eggs. Rather he said that God would "give the Holy Spirit to those who ask him." The Holy Spirit is more precious than food.

How should we live our daily lives as people who have gone down to death with Christ and risen with him? We should live in the Holy Spirit, God's Spirit that surrounds us and is available for the asking. The Spirit is in the hands of friends who help us. The Spirit is in the face of strangers who wake us to our new selves and to new duties. The Spirit is in the arms of Christians gathered to comfort and strengthen one another. The Spirit is in the words of Scripture, in literature that penetrates the ambiguities of life, in poetry that takes us to the heights and depths. The Spirit takes some form in every case of our need when we attempt to sanctify the lives we lead.

We are about to sing a wonderful old hymn about being in the resurrected state right now: "It Is Well with My Soul." When sorrows in this life roll like billows of the sea, the Spirit is peace like a river that carries us through. When temptations come, as surely they will, when it seems as if the evil and injustice against which we contend has Satanic force, the Spirit assures us that Jesus has come through it all before us.

My friends, as we are about to baptize Naomi Fassil and welcome her into the household of faith, let us be reminded that this is not only a rite of initiation. Nor is it only a symbolic washing away of personal sins—Naomi is far too young to need that kind of bath, and many of us were baptized long before we were old enough to have mastered the art of sinning boldly. When Jesus was baptized by John in the Jordan, he went down into the waters of the primal creation, the voice of God spoke his approval, and the spirit of God descended, just as at the original creation. Jesus rose from his baptism a new person, like a second creation. Let us be reminded today that baptism means that we also have conquered death and come into resurrection. Let us welcome Naomi and live with her the lives of resurrected and holy people. Amen.

2

The Potter's Vessels[1]

Jeremiah 18:1–11; Philemon 1–21; Luke 14:21–33

On behalf of Marsh Chapel let me welcome all the new students who are moving in here this weekend, preparing for matriculation tomorrow and classes the day after. Even more warmly we welcome your parents who are here to help with the move-in. May your aches and pains from carrying books and TV sets temporarily obscure your sadness at losing your children to a university that is separate from your home. Like potters molding clay, you have molded your children until now. From now on, different potters will be at work. The foundational shape you have provided is far more important than anything the academy can do. Yet your children now move into a new world with new potters.

The Bible has many wonderful images for God, who of course in a literal sense is beyond imagination. The central controlling image is that God is creator of heaven and earth, of everything visible and invisible, as the first chapter of Colossians puts it. This is a paradoxical image because it says, in effect, that God literally cannot be imagined. Anything that can be imagined is something *in* heaven or *on* earth, something visible or invisible. That covers everything that is some one thing rather than something else. Anything that can be imagined is something created. The majesty of God the Creator, whose praises we sing, is that everything imaginable derives from God's creation. In everything imaginable, God is present as creator.

---

1. Preached September 5, 2004, the fourteenth Sunday after Pentecost.

But to identify God with any imaginable thing is idolatry. I want to put this point about divine transcendence in the front of our minds as we think about the image of God as a potter.

All the images of God are metaphors and symbols, which means that we make a point in using them, but should not say that they describe God outside the context of making that point. The Psalms say that God is the rock of our salvation, and we know what that means without ever literally thinking that God is a rock to be studied by geologists. The Twenty-Third Psalm says God is a shepherd, and we know what that means without thinking that God runs an agribusiness. When Jeremiah speaks of the hand of God, or Isaiah of the hem of God's robe, or Exodus of Moses seeing God's backside, we know that these are metaphors of a divine body when God is really not a body. Yet we can use those metaphors without flinching or misusing them. When so many books of the Bible imagine God as speaking and mention the Word of God, Jews, Christians, and Muslims sometimes forget that this too is metaphorical. In Exodus, God is imagined as a warrior who leads the Israelites out of Egypt, and in 1 Samuel and other places God is imagined as a king. Hosea spoke of God as a lover with an unfaithful wife. In Job, God is likened to an architect when it comes to laying the foundations of the natural world. Jesus often spoke of the "kingdom of God," and yet he imagined the head of the kingdom as a father rather than a king. Many of the images of God represent God as a person of some sort. And yet John says that God is love, not a lover but love itself. Metaphors like these are necessary to relate the Creator of heaven and earth, all things visible and invisible, to the affairs of human life, and we need to keep track of the contexts in which they apply and those in which they are obviously false in a literal sense.

Jeremiah's image of God as potter has application in the context of God creating and shaping people and nations. In the first chapter of Genesis, the famous first creation story, the natural world arises out of God speaking like a king laying down the law. But in the second chapter of Genesis, more detailed about the creation of human beings, God is imagined to be a potter. God takes mud and molds it into the form of a man, like a ceramic doll, and then breathes into it to bring the doll to life. Saint Paul describes God as a potter, in Romans 9, when he wants to make the point that the creator can do with us what he wants. What do we learn from the image that God is a potter and that we are the potter's vessels?

The chief lesson is that we can look to the things that shape us and see God in them. The hand of God, to use that image, is in all the things that give us life and form. When I was a teenager, I worked in a Scout Camp during the summer and loved to lie out on the parade ground on clear nights when everyone else slept and groove on the stars above. I felt them as my most real and awesome environment. Under the vastness of that sky I was absolutely, ultimately, nakedly myself before God on that hill outside Irondale, Missouri, and I loved God the Creator who made me in that place in the heavens and earth. One such night, knowing that I was already God's because I lay within the potter's hands, I decided that the way to be myself in God was to be a minister. Many of you too, I suspect, find yourselves most cosmically and intimately shaped by such experiences of God as the one who places you within the vastness of creation.

Many other parts of nature shape us as well, and thereby reveal how the Potter-Creator works. We are not clay, yet we have evolved out of the elemental physical properties of the earth. Our blood is about as salty as the ocean from which our distant ancestors emerged. Humans are social beings, and the history of society and civilization is part of the shaping process. Our own communities are powerful forces for shaping us with cultures that make us somewhat akin and somewhat different. A few minutes ago I alluded to the ways our families shape us, like a potter giving us form. We are also shaped by our friends and enemies, our schools and work, and by the accidents of history during our watch. The technical theological term for all these formative influences is "prevenient grace." God is to be found in all the things that "come before" and shape us.

Jeremiah reminds us of the downside of this, however, namely, that sometimes the pots do not turn out well and the potter has to remake them. Planets collide and suns flame out. The natural evolution of the human species was at the cost of countless species that died out; maintenance of human metabolism requires enormous expenditures of the energies of other things. Human societies make high civilization possible, but they also do horribly unjust things. Families are not perfect, and friends sometimes lead us into great harm and evil. Christians believe that everyone is born and shaped with flaws.

Christians also believe, however, that everyone can be repaired like a pot thrown back onto the wheel to be reshaped. This too happens in many ways as people learn what is right and wrong and events force serious judgments on behavior. Institutions of moral and spiritual education are in every civilization, and they all can be construed as agencies of the divine Potter, more grace.

The specifically Christian agency for the repair of broken vessels is discipleship to Jesus Christ. Our gospel text from Luke indicates that this is no small thing indeed! Discipleship requires total commitment. Jesus says that potential disciples need to count the cost beforehand to see whether they want to enter onto the Christian path. Luke quotes him as saying that "Whoever comes to me and does not hate father and mother, wife and children, brothers and sisters, yes, and even life itself, cannot be my disciple." These are extremely sharp words and run directly against Jesus's message emphasized elsewhere that we should love all these people, and strangers as well. In Matthew's version of this saying, Jesus says that whoever loves their relatives more than they love Jesus cannot be his disciples, not that they actually have to hate their relatives. Nevertheless, Matthew quotes Jesus as saying he has not come to bring peace but a sword and that being his disciple will in fact set people against their families.

Jesus's point, I believe, is that for us to repair our broken lives we need to attach ourselves wholeheartedly to his way of living in a community of love. This does not mean that we have to leave our families or friends—these are the sources of our strengths. But sometimes our families, friends, and social habits are the very cause of our failings and we need to go back to basics. We need to accept being thrown back onto the potter's wheel to be reshaped. The Christian life day by day is lived on the potter's wheel, always in process of being reshaped. This means always hunting for means of grace to be better vessels, better people. The technical theological term for this is "sanctification." As we seek out and live among the shaping influences of sanctifying grace, we are able to reestablish relations with family and friends, bringing out the best in all. Flawed children from broken homes in an urban ghetto can be made whole and new by a long trip to the country where they can lie on their backs at night under the stars and feel that God creates even them, along with all the points of light. Prodigal sinners can return to their homes and find love that makes them new. Confused young people can come to the university and find the gracious love of learning that turns them away from their own problems to serve the world and God. The comforting thing about being a broken vessel is that even the flawed pot is part of God's creation. Creation continues until all are redeemed, every broken vessel.

Now I invite you to Jesus's table to partake in the ancient meal that feeds the soul and heals it when distressed. Come to this table to feel the Creator's grace that shapes us through the heavens and the earth. Come to this table that inherits all the graceful powers of civilization. Come to this table where families are purified and fulfilled as the family of Jesus. Come to this table where the comfort of God can be felt in every influence of the Potter's hand. Come to this table to find your own work as a divine influence on your friends and world. Come to this table, a potter's wheel, where you can become a perfect vessel of the divine Potter. In Jesus' name, come. Amen.

3

The Value of Something Lost[1]

Jeremiah 4:11–12, 21–28; Psalm 14;
1 Timothy 1:11–17; Luke 15:1–10

New people in Boston know a great deal about getting lost. Those of you new to the University this academic year surely must have noticed that many streets do not have name signs. Sometimes, if you're traveling down a street, the cross streets will be named, but not the one you are on. If you do by chance know the name of the street you are on, it might not last because likely the name changes every few blocks. And if you ask a native how to get to the Boston Library, for instance, they will say, "Go past Kenmore Square to Copley Square and it's across from Trinity Church." If you protest that you don't know where the squares are or how to get from one to the other or what Trinity Church looks like, they'll say this means you probably are not from Boston, a misfortune from which you might not recover. The only remedy I know for being lost in Boston is to root for the Red Sox through enough near-miss seasons as to enter into total mental empathy with native fans who know how to get from Fenway Park to anywhere.

Jesus's point in the gospel reading from Luke was not about being lost, although that too would be worth a sermon, but about losing something you value and the effort you expend on finding it. In our text he told two parables. One was about the shepherd who lost one sheep and left all the others to go after it. He risked ninety-nine sheep for the sake of finding the

1. Preached September 12, 2004, the fifteenth Sunday after Pentecost.

lost one. The second parable was about a woman with only ten coins who scours her house to find one that is lost. She did not risk her nine remaining coins to find the lost one, but she worked hard to find it. In both cases, Jesus emphasized the great joy that comes from finding what is lost, a greater joy than enjoying what was not lost. He editorialized on both parables by saying there is greater joy in heaven for the recovery of a sinner than for all the righteous people who are not lost. People who think of themselves as righteous are always uncomfortable with these parables.

Jesus knew about this discomfort, of course. Immediately following our reading today in Luke is the parable of the Prodigal Son. As you know in that story, a father loses his younger son who wanted to leave home and seek his fortune; the son squanders away his fortune in riotous living (not at all like going away to college, you understand), and he returns home to be a slave in his father's house. The father receives him with the greatest possible joy, dresses him in the best robes, and kills a fatted calf to give him a party. It was like finding the lost sheep, the lost coin, but far more joyous because it was the father's child. It was like heaven rejoicing at the salvation of the sinner. Then the elder brother comes in from the field where he had been working and throws a fit at the festivities for his brother. He complains he has worked like a slave all his life for his father who has never once given him a party, not even a goat, let alone a fatted calf. He refuses to come in, and the father goes out to mollify him, saying that the elder son would be his inheritor and that he too should welcome his brother home because the boy had been dead and was brought back to life. Jesus stopped the story there and did not say whether the elder brother ever came in to accept his brother, or his father's love.

The most dramatic part of the parable of the Prodigal Son is that it has no ending. So we are prodded to ask, what is the story really about? It is not only about the prodigal who lost his wealth and came crawling back to heaven. Nor is it really only about the loving father who accepted him back and rejoiced more over his return than over his long-suffering eldest son. The parable is about the righteous elder brother who lost his innocence: he was jolted to discover that his years of righteous obedience and service to his father were morally ambiguous, motivated in part by selfishness and pride in being superior to his brother, not only by the love he protested.

In Luke's Gospel, the parables of the Lost Sheep, the Lost Coin, and the Lost Son go together. Just before those parables, Jesus had been addressing a large crowd of his disciples, and just afterward he returned to addressing his disciples. But these three parables, in chapter 15, are addressed to Pharisees and scribes who had been criticizing him for socializing with known sinners. The Pharisees and scribes were like the elder brother, representing the tradition of faithfulness and strict observance of religious obedience in the large household of Jewish faith, of which Jesus and his disciples were members. What kind of righteous people could they be to object to Jesus ministering to sinners? On the other hand, what is the point of righteousness if the recovery of sinners is so much more important than the congratulations of the righteous? Why should anyone be righteous, they might ask, if it is better to be a sinner and repent in the nick of time?

The answer, of course, is that you should be righteous, not for the reward or congratulations, but because that is the righteous thing to be. The proper motive for righteousness is in the righteousness of the deed, not in having an identity with status. When the motive for righteousness is to have an identity that prides itself in being better than the identity of sinners, then the moral ambiguity of that righteousness corrupts the righteousness itself. Taking pride in one's righteousness is an innocence well lost.

Americans these days know something about this kind of loss of innocence. No matter what you think about the upcoming presidential election, things are vastly changed since the presidential campaign four years ago. The United States now occupies two countries that did not attack us or provide a greater threat to American security than any number of other countries. This was justified by a new doctrine of "preemptive war," which everyone knows deep down is just another name for a war of aggression when no immediate threat is present. So the American innocent sense of being the righteous defender of peace and justice is made ambiguous by our occupation of foreign territory.

In the grief and confusion after 9/11, the third anniversary of which we remembered yesterday, the government made the perhaps understandable mistake of declaring a *"war* on terrorism." War is what you fight to conquer or hold territory and control a government. Terrorists duck when attacked and hold no territory, and they govern no peoples except themselves. What was needed was a massive international police action against the criminal terrorists. But misled by the rhetoric of war, we attacked and conquered Afghanistan instead, driving out an admittedly bad Taliban government, which no more could control al-Qaeda than Mr. Karzai's puppet government can. We pray that Mr. Karzai's government can bring stability, but al-Qaeda still flourishes in the hills, as do the Taliban forces; the tribal leaders, whom our press calls warlords, have more power than the central government.

In respect of Iraq, our government either deceived itself or attempted to deceive the nation about connections with al-Qaeda and weapons of mass destruction. Surely someone in the government knew how terrible war is and should have insisted on making certain about the need to go to war before doing so. Some Americans believe the government deliberately lied about its motives for war, and others believe it was only incompetent with regard to intelligence. In either case, Americans' traditional innocent pride in their government has become morally ambiguous.

Our soldiers, for the most part, have fought valiantly, taking care to minimize civilian casualties where possible, and coping with the shock of being hated by many people whom they thought they were liberating. Both presidential candidates call for outcomes that would make it the case that our fallen soldiers are not dying in vain. Would to God that were so! The same thing must be said for the Iraqi soldiers who died under the rain of our bombs. No soldier's death should be in vain. But what else could those deaths be but vain in some very profound sense, if the war should not have been fought in the first place? Deep down, everyone knows this, and the attempts to find something good to come out of the war only confuse the nation's tortured conscience.

Our country has so lost its innocence that it seems to be more sharply divided than at any time since the Civil War. Deep down everyone knows the sad tale I've sketched, though it is told with many spins. Some people so sharply mourn the loss of innocence and life that they insist our course must have been right somehow, despite the evidence, and are ready to believe anything that reinforces that view. Other people are so angered at the loss of innocence that they rage that their righteous nation has been stolen from them. Debates about economic, environmental, and welfare policies occupy a lot of middle ground. Even the so-called culture wars of the last two decades were fought over a broad middle ground. But the sad tale of American military adventures has so divided the country that even our sense of being a united people has been made ambiguous. Honest and wise people differ over where to go from here, and no easy solutions present themselves. What is certain is that, wherever we go, it will be without the innocence we felt four years ago.

Without suggesting anything about what Jesus might say concerning the wars in Afghanistan and Iraq, I do believe that Jesus would say our loss of innocence is a good thing. You can lose a sheep and find it again. You can recover a lost coin. You can even have an estranged child return to you. All of these losses recouped are like divine joy at the redemption of sinners. The deeper meaning of Jesus's parables here, however, has to do with the false righteousness of the Pharisees and scribes, as Luke describes them. Their sense of moral superiority blinded them to the value of Jesus associating with sinners. In a like manner, the accursed innocence of American false righteousness has blinded us to the necessity to work for peace and justice, prosperity and security, with sinners, among whom we are.

We struggle to transcend partisanship and hear the gospel in the turmoil of our divided politics. Where is the Holy Spirit in the political racket? I believe at least four promptings of the Spirit can be discerned.

First and most obviously, we need to respect, honor, and love those with whom we disagree. When no common ground can be identified, this is difficult, especially when the dispute is fueled by grief and anger. But we all have the common ground of loss of innocence, whether we admit or deny it, with the consequence that we have to work together to make the best of a morally ambiguous situation.

Second, the gospel prompts us through the Golden Rule systematically to look at ourselves from the perspectives of those who oppose us. This means we each must empathize with all the divided perspectives within American politics. More importantly, it means we must look at America through the eyes of its opponents: our "insurgents" are their "freedom fighters"; our "liberation" is their "foreign occupation." Christians especially should aim for a God's-eye view, and God sees through every perspective, loving all the sinners on all sides.

Third, the gospel prompts us to be with and help the people who are hurt; the grieving families of fallen soldiers (on all sides); the civilians maimed or grieved; the economies shaken; the elderly, sick, and uneducated whose lives could have been improved were it not for the cost of our wars. Irrespective of political or national stance, each hurting person is like a lost sheep or an estranged child for whom we have responsibility. Every bombed house is someone's lost coin.

Fourth, the Spirit insists we must come to terms with our loss of innocence. We can ask forgiveness of our own failings in the measure we forgive others. We can be wise about policies only when we are transparently honest. We can go forward only if we know the costs will be high and the outcomes ambiguous. And as redeemed sinners, we cannot under any circumstances back away from the hard issues on our watch just because we know we might fail or do evil in some respects even as we win for the good in others.

The gospel calls us to love the whole creation, despite its ambiguities and pains. The Christian way to the joy of heaven is through the wilderness of crosses. This is a hard lesson for students, especially new ones, who, like the grieving and angry, want a clear path to righteousness. Let me invite you, however, into the company of redeemed sinners whose innocence is lost, the company of Pharisees and scribes who have heard and understood Jesus's parables. In this company, the griefs and rages of ambiguous life can be borne with heavenly joy. May God receive and bless us all. Amen.

4

Living in Our Own Time[1]

Jeremiah 32:1—3a, 1—15; 2 Samuel 11:27b—12:9; Luke 16:11—31

The gospel from Luke is one of the most colorful stories in the Bible and it has a vivid history in Christian art and imagination. The rich man is known as Dives, although that is just a Latin word for "rich man." The images in the story that Jesus used for hell and heaven are not typical of the Hebrew Bible. For most of the Hebrew Bible, hell or Sheol is a shady place where all souls go and gradually dissipate. Ecclesiastes pointed out that the rich and the poor, the good and the evil, all go to the same place and amount to vanity. A strong tradition of thought in ancient Israel was that God is the God of the living, not the dead, and that people who handle dead bodies are unclean and need to be purified. This tradition was more or less well represented in Jesus's time by the party of the Sadducees, which included the priests who superintended the Temple worship. You will remember the incident recounted in the twentieth chapter of Luke where the Sadducees tried to trick Jesus with a question about whose wife a woman would be in heaven if she had married each of seven brothers. The Sadducees themselves did not believe in the resurrection and thought this question revealed the contradictory nature of belief in a heavenly afterlife. Jesus answered that in heaven people would not have sexual identities and would be like angels. He then reinterpreted the claim that God is the God of the living by citing Moses's name for God, namely, the God of Abraham, Isaac,

---

1. Preached September 26, 2004, the seventeenth Sunday after Pentecost.

and Jacob: if God is the God of the living, then in Moses's time, Abraham, Isaac, and Jacob must still be alive in some afterlife.

In contrast to the Israelite belief that souls just fade away in Sheol, a tradition of immortality or resurrection grew up in Jewish thought during Hellenistic times, that is, after Alexander the Great conquered the area and brought in Greek culture about three centuries before Jesus. In Jesus's day, this was represented by the party of the Pharisees, and Jesus was a theological Pharisee in this and other matters. The logic of this position was something like this. If the soul is naturally immortal, or all souls are resurrected from the dead, then the righteousness of God's kingdom requires that in the afterlife the good souls must go to heaven and the bad souls to everlasting hellish punishment. In early Christian thought, some people believed that every soul is naturally immortal and therefore has to go someplace, to heaven or hell. Other early Christians believed that only the saved believers would be resurrected to be with God and Christ while the unsaved would simply remain dead with no resurrection at all. The Greek philosophical idea of natural immortality became more influential in later Christian thought so that by the time of the Middle Ages most people were convinced that every soul survived and had to go somewhere after death. In addition to heaven and hell, which rewarded good or bad people, the medievals imagined limbo for unbaptized children who had died before the age of responsibility and purgatory for the people who were bad but could be made good by some eons of torture. Most of us today would doubt the benefits of eons of purgatorial torture. Jesus's image of heaven for Lazarus and hell for Dives was not quite as elaborate as the medieval imagery, but lay in that line of development.

Now we do not know whether Jesus's image of heaven and hell in our text was what he really believed, or was a metaphorical appeal to the popular imagination for the sake of telling his story. His more usual image of last things was that God would cataclysmically come down from heaven into history, punishing the evildoers, rewarding the just, and setting up a global kingdom of justice with Jesus as its head. On this account Jesus would return to history and reshape it, although he also believed in treasure in heaven. I myself suspect that Jesus's vivid picture of Dives in hell looking up at Lazarus in heaven, resting in the bosom of Abraham as the spiritual says, was intended as something of a literary device for making his point.

Note that Jesus did not say that Lazarus was a particularly good man. Nor did he say that the rich man Dives was particularly bad. We are left to infer that the sin of Dives was that he did not pay attention the poor man at his gates. Jewish religious law was quite clear that the wealthy have a responsibility of charity to the poor. Presumably, Dives's brothers also were rich but callous, which is why he worried about their fate. The power of Jesus's story is that its very picture of sumptuous wealth juxtaposed to crippling poverty brings to our mind, like a physical perception, the fundamental injustice of such disparities in wealth where the rich don't care for the poor. You don't need the law, or even an editorial comment, to see that it was wrong for Dives to feast sumptuously every day while beggars sought his crumbs with the dogs. It was up to Dives to do something about that. We can just see that.

Americans can see the point of Jesus's parable even when it is hard to see that we are the rich people of the earth while others scramble for the crumbs our global economy leaves them. Even poor Americans are rich by global standards. Remember that King David did not seem to see much wrong in seducing Bathsheba, the wife of Uriah the Hittite, and then sending Uriah to the front lines to be killed in battle. Then Nathan, his prophet, told him about a rich man with many sheep who took his poor neighbor's only and beloved sheep so he could give a banquet. David as royal judge condemned the rich man, and Nathan told him, "you are that man." David got the point.

American global capitalism increases the world's wealth and make many people richer. But it stomps those who cannot compete well. We blame noncompetitive people for their own poverty and noncapitalist culture that makes them noncompetitive. Our economic system increases the gap between the competitive and noncompetitive, and demands that the noncompetitive people give up their native cultures to enter the shallow, rat-race culture of competitive wealth seeking. If Jesus's parable causes us to just see that Dives should be condemned, Jesus tells us Americans, "you are that man."

Please understand that I am not against capitalism, nor against Dives dressing and eating well. The point is that we and Dives have a responsibility to the poor on our global doorstep, especially those whose poverty is accentuated by the system that provides our wealth. Capitalism, or any other economic system, is morally tolerable only when it cares for the losers. The deceptive mythology of capitalism, alas, likens economic competition to a sporting competition: the winners deserve to win by virtue of being better, and the losers deserve to lose precisely because they are less competitive.

In real economic life, however, why should losing to the Haliburtons of the world mean that your people deserve to be poor and dependent on crumbs? Lazarus no less than Dives is a child of God.

Now all of these points make good sermon material, and I hope you take them to heart. But notice that Jesus took the story in another direction. He said there was a great gulf fixed between heaven and hell that could not be crossed: no purgatory or limbo for Jesus! What you do in this life is what counts. Moreover, when Dives begged Abraham to send someone risen from the dead to warn his brothers, Abraham replied that Moses had laid down the moral standards, the brothers knew that, and this should be enough. You see, Jesus's real point was not about the geography of heaven and hell. He concocted that scene to draw attention to the irreversible and absolute moral significance of what we do in this life. It is not what we shall do in some heavenly or hellish afterlife that counts. Our worth consists in how we live in our own time. The scene of Lazarus in the bosom of Abraham and Dives in torment was Jesus's imaginative expression of the worth of their respective lives. He said that the worth of those lives cannot be changed after they die.

What does this imply for us? First, it means that what we believe about the geography of the afterlife is not important one way or another so long as we get Jesus's point: we stand under judgment for what we do and are in this life. Unlike Dives, who seems to have been oblivious to any absolute judgment on his life, we should live with a consciousness that what we do now has ultimate significance for who we are before God. The danger in afterlife thinking is that we are tempted to postpone taking our lives seriously. Jesus turned afterlife thinking around to say, "Be serious here and now." Not later but now we live under divine judgment. Now our lives have ultimate significance for defining our worth.

A second implication is that we should therefore attend to the issues that arise on our watch with utmost seriousness. The poor are on our doorstep: what can we do about them now? Countless other issues in addition to poverty shape the moral contours of our environment. Dealing with them all is how we live in our own time.

The Christian gospel is that no matter how good we are now and throughout our lives before God, it is never good enough. Yet God loves us anyway and receives us with mercy, restoring us to good standing. But now, being restored, we have no excuse for not amending our lives and pursuing the holiness of justice and mercy in the way we live in our own time. Christianity says that Dives can be changed in his own lifetime.

So I invite you to take your life in our time with ultimate seriousness, knowing that this is the life you have to lead and none other. I invite you to accept the grace of God in Christ to give you the power of righteousness while you still have this life to lead. I invite you to look at the world around you and make a difference for justice. Help the poor, improve the economy, oppose the selfish, put peace ahead of control, treat your enemies as you would be treated, protect nature as God's creation, cherish friends as God cherishes you, create high culture and a decent society because you are creators in God's image, forgive because God forgives, renew others because God renews, love everyone and everything because God does, and live your life now with the laughter and joy of absolute seriousness because this is the life God gives you. Amen.

5

Religion for Reward[1]

Lamentations 1:1–6; 2 Timothy 1:1–4; Luke 17:1–10

Today's gospel from Luke disturbs our sensibilities because of its suppositions about slavery. Jesus refers to slavery as an accepted institution of society and does not speak against it. Moreover, he assumes that many of his listeners themselves have slaves and that they know how to treat them. You would insist, he says, that your slave finish serving you with evening food and drink, even after a long day in the field, before time off for his or her own dinner. Jesus approves the rather harsh and uncompromising treatment of slaves and uses that to make his point about the behavior he expects from the disciples.

This passage has not always been disturbing. It was one of the principal defenses of slavery in Christianity down to the 1860s in the United States. For much of Christian history, slavery did not need to be defended at all because everyone took it for granted. Jesus's own statement needs to be understood in terms of the social situation of the ancient world, in which slavery was indeed an accepted practice. People could become slaves by being on the losing side in a war, by being sold into slavery by their parents, or by selling themselves into slavery because they otherwise lacked the means to take care of themselves. The children of slaves were slaves. The economies of most Mediterranean societies required slave labor. Much slave labor was menial and some was sexually abusive, but sometimes slaves rose to

---

1. Preached October 3, 2004, the eighteenth Sunday after Pentecost.

positions of great responsibility. Slavery in the ancient world did not have especially racial or ethnic connotations except in cases where the enslaved losers in a war were racially or ethnically different from the winners. The Hebrew Bible laid down some rules for the humane treatment of slaves but did not condemn the practice. Saint Paul encouraged slaves to be obedient to their masters and in one instance persuaded a runaway slave to return to his master and his master to receive him back as a Christian, though still a slave. He did not suggest abolishing slavery or even that individual Christians should free their slaves.

While it was clear in the ancient world that many slaves were intelligent and responsible, there was also the belief that some people are "natural slaves," that is, people in need of others to watch out for them while they do work within a limited sphere. Aristotle, for instance, believed that all women are by nature "natural slaves" and need men to take care of them, although they can manage a household. Without using slavery language for women, Saint Paul believed that they needed to be subordinated to and taken care of by men, despite the plain evidence before his eyes that some women were paramount leaders in their congregations.

One part of Hellenistic and Roman culture that seems strange to us is the extent to which all human relations were seen in terms of dominance and submission. Relations among social classes were defined in terms of dominance and submission, and the relations between slave owners and slaves were part of this. Sexual relations could not be conceived as equal, only as a matter of domination and submission. The flip side of the dominance and submission theme in the ancient Greco-Roman world was that everyone except the emperor was supposed to be on the lookout for who his or her lord or master is, so as to be of service.

In our time almost no one would believe slavery to be morally tolerable, except perhaps in Africa where it is still practiced in some places. In our time, we are somewhat divided about whether men should dominate women. Most secular Western societies have adopted equal women's rights, and mainline religions have gone along with that. Many evangelical Protestants, however, as well as Roman Catholics and Orthodox Christians, hold to the biblical injunctions to keep women in subordinate roles to men.

How should Christians respond to biblical assumptions about cultural matters that are in direct contradiction to what we have come to believe, for good reason, to be the moral course? We should look very carefully at the moral distance between the ancient world and our own. Just as we would not accept ancient science over against our own, so we should not accept ancient social customs regarding slavery or gender relations when we have come to know better. The Bible's deep principle of the equality of all people as children of God contradicts many of the social customs that the Bible accepted uncritically, even if biblical writers had not drawn out that implication. Jesus's own practice of treating women with great respect and near equality stood in contrast to the social expectations of his time. The implication of equal dignity for all persons has been drawn out abundantly in the last four centuries and we now believe in human rights; in Christian societies, that belief comes from the biblical principles of love and equality. We need not hold it against the prophets, Paul, or Jesus, that they failed to see the full social implications of the claim that God loves all people as equally divine children and that relations among people should be those of mutual love, to which slavery is a contradiction.

Nevertheless, though our sensibilities are rightly disturbed by Jesus's positive use of slavery to make a point, we should still attempt to see the point he was making. His point was not about the institution of slavery at all. It was about duty to God that applies to everyone. Just as the ancient world believed that slaves owed perfect obedience to their masters and should not be rewarded extra for merely doing their duty, so everyone should be obedient to God and not get extra credit for being so. We do not enter life on a morally neutral playing field, where opportunities await for doing good that we can take up if we want some special reward, but that we can also simply ignore if we don't want the reward. No. We are already defined by our obligations. To accept and engage those obligations is simply what is expected of us.

Jesus's point in this analogy with slavery was to attack spiritual materialism. In his influential book *Cutting through Spiritual Materialism*, the Tibetan Buddhist theologian and missionary to America Chogyam Trungpa defined spiritual materialism as the ego's use of religion to enhance its own gratification. In Buddhist cultures this often meant attaining spiritual powers so that others would look up to you. In Western and many third-world cultures many people think they should be religious and moral only for the sake of getting to heaven, a place of high rewards. Good Christians are also prone to a kind of spiritual materialism that sees holiness as an ultimate ego gratification. Jesus's point was that we should do our duty to God and neighbors just because it is our duty. The moral issues of our watch define us, and how we do our duty defines our moral worth, set in the context of God's forgiveness and mercy. The proper motive for religious practice should be for its own sake, not for the sake of some reward.

Our proper relation to God, as you know, is astonishingly complicated, consisting in part of awe and reverence for the glory of the Creator, in part of gratitude for our lives and the bounty of creation, in part of confession of our sins and grateful reception of divine forgiveness, and in part of learning to love God as our Ultimate Beloved despite the fact God gives us unfair lives, unlovely neighbors, pain, and death. Relations with our neighbors are partial versions of our proper relation to the Ultimate Ground of our Being. This complex religious life of holiness is extremely difficult, but it is not for the sake of anything except itself. To learn to live in holy awe, gratitude, repentance, and love collectively is the end and goal of life. Should some mastery of awe, gratitude, repentance, and love win respect from our neighbors or an afterlife in heaven is wholly beside the point, and the ego-lure of social respect or heaven is likely to corrupt the true Christian path to which we are ordered. Jesus said, "So you also, when you have done all that you were ordered to do, say 'We are worthless slaves; we have done only what we ought to have done!'"

Jesus, of course, was the "worthless" slave, as Paul said in Philippians 2, whose humility so perfected his relation with God that all of us who follow him into the duty of that slavery can come to holy awe, ultimate gratitude, repentant redemption, and the love that perfects human nature. I invite you to the table of Jesus where the slaves come for nourishment so that they can do their whole duty to God and neighbor. Come to the table where God's glory suffuses humble food, and be in awe. Come to the table where Christ's presence incarnates God in creation, and be filled with gratitude. Come to the table with confession in your heart to receive the blessed grace of forgiveness, and be empowered to live the unstoppable life of redeemed sinners. Come to the table where the true host is your beloved, and love God as a perfect lover. Come. Amen

6

A New Covenant[1]

Jeremiah 31:21–34; 2 Timothy 3:11—4:5; Luke 18:1–8

No greater homecoming can be imagined than Jeremiah's prediction of a new covenant between God and Israel. The old covenant, given to Moses on Mount Sinai, was written down. It had to be read to the people and the people had to study it. The old covenant required leaders who could interpret it to the people. Moreover, the people broke the Mosaic covenant, despite the fact that God was their "husband," as Jeremiah's text says. The old covenant was like a marriage, and the people, the "wife," had been unfaithful. With the new covenant, however, everyone would have the proper ways to behave toward God, and the faithfulness to do so, engraved on their hearts. Religious faithfulness would be virtually automatic in all Israel because God would internalize it as the source of their actions, not as an option for action. Israel would not need to seek and defend a homeland with God as a liberating mediator. God would come home to Israel.

A little background about Jeremiah helps understand this text. The kingdom of the twelve tribes of Israel that David had united lasted only through the reign of his son, Solomon. After that it was divided into a northern kingdom, which took the name Israel, and a southern kingdom called Judah, which contained the capital Jerusalem and was mainly the territory of the tribe of Judah. In our text, Jeremiah calls these kingdoms the

---

1. Preached October 17, 2004, the twentieth Sunday after Pentecost, and Homecoming Sunday at the University.

A New Covenant

house of Israel and the house of Judah respectively. Israel and Judah were caught politically between the great empires of Assyria in the north and Egypt in the south. For the most part they were bound as vassals to Assyria, that is, Iraq, but chafed and rebelled against the tribute they were required to pay. Israel, the Northern Kingdom, was utterly defeated in 722/21 BCE and its leadership deported to Assyria. That was the end of Israel. Through the next century, Judah maintained its balance by appealing to Egypt against Assyria. Assyria overextended itself, however, and was defeated in 612 BCE by the Babylonians, also in today's Iraq. In 605 BCE the Babylonian king Nebuchadnezzar decisively defeated the Egyptian Pharaoh Neco at Carchemish, and Judah was fully under the thumb of Babylon. In 597 BCE Nebuchadnezzar took Jerusalem and deported the king, Jehoiakim, to Babylon, installing a puppet king in his place, Zedekiah. Zedekiah tried to revolt in 587 BCE, and Nebuchadnezzar returned and razed Jerusalem to the ground, destroying the temple and taking the remaining aristocracy and perhaps many other Jews to Babylon. The prophet Ezekiel had gone to Babylon in 597 BCE with the exiles, and Jeremiah fled to Egypt in 587 BCE. As things turned out, about fifty years later the Persians, that is, the present-day Iranians, defeated the Babylonians, the Iraqis, and allowed some of the Babylonian Jews to return to Jerusalem to set up a new puppet kingdom and rebuild the temple. (As you can see, the twenty-first-century conflicts in the Middle East had their origins in the ancient Near East, with the addition of the Muslim Arabs in the seventh century of the Common Era and the Americans in the twentieth.)

Jeremiah was called to be a prophet when he was but a boy, in 627 BCE, while Josiah was king of Judah. Israel had been destroyed for nearly a century, but Josiah reconquered some of its territory while the Assyrians were dealing with the Babylonians. Jeremiah came from a priestly family and served in the court of Zedekiah, the last king of Judah, between 597 and 587, who rebelled against the Babylonians, contrary to Jeremiah's advice. The text of Jeremiah's prophecy is chronologically scrambled, with bits from his forty years of prophecy mixed around. Usually we can tell from events referred to when most of the passages were written, however. You will note in our text today that Jeremiah predicts that God will help both the house of Israel and the house of Judah, having destroyed them. This means that this passage is not an early writing when only Israel was destroyed but a late writing when both were destroyed, possibly after 597 when Judah first lost to Nebuchadnezzar or perhaps around 587 when the whole city was razed.

Now Jeremiah's main problem was this: God had promised to protect Israel and to keep David's descendants on the throne forever, even if they were not faithful. But in his lifetime Jeremiah saw things go from bad to worse with the final destruction of the remaining portion of David's kingdom. How could a priest and prophet of Yahweh explain this? Jeremiah's answer, like that of the other prophets, was that the people of Israel had themselves broken the covenant and that their political troubles were God's punishment for this, like an angry husband punishing a wayward wife. Jeremiah also said, however, that God would restore Israel and Judah after punishing them, "sowing [them] with the seed of humans and the seed of animals," as our text put it. Several weeks ago the lectionary reading from Jeremiah was about his investing in property to show confidence that Judah's fortunes would be restored. In today's text he says that God will give a new covenant in which God's law is within the hearts of the people.

Of course he lost his investment with the destruction of Israel. Although the Persians did restore the Jewish aristocracy to Jerusalem and let them build the Second Temple, Judah was always a puppet state, first of the Persians, then of the Greeks under Alexander, then of the Romans as at the time of Christ and lasting until the Muslim conquest in the seventh century. The secular State of Israel was established by the European powers in the mid-twentieth century but has maintained itself albeit as a client-state of America ever since. This was not what Jeremiah had in mind as the restoration of the house of Israel and the house of Judah.

Nor did the new covenant ever take place in the sense of writing the law of God on people's hearts rather than on scrolls. There were brief periods of Torah purification, as in the days of Ezra and Nehemiah who built the Second Temple under the Persians, but these were very much an external application of the law, not an exhibition of its internal shaping of the human heart. Saint Paul, in the second chapter of his letter to the Romans, describes conscience as a kind of law written on the heart, but applies it to Gentiles in contrast to Jews who have the much clearer external written law, and notes that both Jews and Gentiles often fail the law. When Jesus and Paul spoke of a new covenant in the Christian sense, it seemed to be quite different from what Jeremiah had in mind.

How then should we understand Jeremiah's failed prophecy of a new covenant that would restore Israel's political fortunes and secure the faithfulness of the people? It is tempting to think a thought that the ancient prophets would never allow, namely, that it is God who was unfaithful to the covenant and its promises. Some Jewish theologians after the Holocaust argued something like this: nothing the Jewish people might have done wrong could possibly justify the horrors of the Holocaust, and therefore there is no God, or God lied in the promises to protect the chosen people, or God is unfaithful or impotent in the face of evil. Surely this response is understandable. Christians have a similar problem regarding divine promises when Jesus did not return after a very short time, sometime within the lifetime of Paul, as Paul thought. As the years went by without Jesus's second coming, the early Christians temporized with remarks that a day of God's time is like a thousand years of ours. But that strategy of indefinite postponement dulls the edge of urgency about salvation, and requires repeated and always arbitrary claims that the apocalypse is really tomorrow. The better understanding is to say, with John, Ephesians, and Colossians, that salvation is already here if we but have the eyes to see it.

The problem, of course, is that if we conceive of God only as a very large spiritual person who makes promises and acts in history, the actual course of history refutes the claims of the prophets and apostles. God is not a big person, however, despite the imagery to that effect throughout the Bible. God is the creator of everything that can be imagined, and this includes persons. As creator, God transcends persons and spirits, as well as nature. You might want to say, with many theologians, that God is thus a superperson, a more-than-personal person. This is fine, so long as you do not say that God makes promises and behaves in history in a faithless way. Our theology must be deeper than this.

One clue for making it deeper is contained in the Jeremiah text. "In those days they shall no longer say: 'The parents have eaten sour grapes, and the children's teeth are set on edge.' But all shall die for their own sins." In other words, people are individually responsible for what they do. One generation cannot do something that legitimately calls forth punishment on the next, nor can the sins of leaders justify punishment of the people. Ezekiel says much the same thing in the eighteenth chapter of his prophetic book. Although both prophets still accounted for Israel's disastrous political fortunes by ascribing to them corporate guilt, they also saw that true justice needs to be tied to personal responsibility. This was the beginning of the insight that justice is defined by secular responsibility, personal and social, not by a large cosmic drama in which God is a principal player who turns out to be fickle.

A second clue to a deeper theology is in the parable from Luke about the corrupt judge who is finally swayed by the repeated insistence of the widow for justice. In Jesus's parable, the corrupt judge is the analogue for God. I would not go so far as to say that Jesus would agree with my view that God should not be depicted as making promises. Nevertheless, he did not draw back from his analogy. The point of his analogy is that we should continually demand justice even when it seems that the controlling powers, ultimately God, are corrupt. The constancy of the demands for justice ultimately wears down a cosmos that seems to reward corruption, violence, power politics, imperial ambitions, and greed. Whereas the widow was seeking just judgment in a lawsuit, our demands for justice cry against poverty, oppression, terrorism, genocide, disenfranchisement, disrespect of other cultures, the sending of soldiers to fight unjust wars, and the failure to pray for enemies who resist unjustified attack and occupation. Whereas the widow needed someone else to give her justice, our demands for justice take the form of committing ourselves to its achievement, so far as we can, even to the point of sacrifice. This parable in Luke immediately follows Jesus's prediction that God would come to separate those who practice righteousness from those who will be left for dead. "Where the corpse is, there the vultures will gather," he said about those who do not pursue justice. When it seemed that injustice has all the power, Jesus told his disciples this "parable about their need to pray always and not to lose heart," as our text began.

Here is our Christian new covenant, which might indeed be a deeper meaning of Jeremiah's. The great Creator God is not like a superking who fixes up history so that we win, or who magically transforms our hearts to perfection. Jesus, however, shows us that the way through history's injustices is through a commitment to righteousness that leads up the cross today to resurrection into new life. And in that resurrected life, day by day, our hearts can be transformed into a holiness from which righteousness does spring as naturally as love. So I invite you into a Christian new covenant that gently transforms Jeremiah's utopian vision into a realism of commitment in the face of adversity, with confidence that new life comes out of defeat when commitment is unshaken and that with a Spirit of mercy and encouragement leads toward a perfection of heart. The invitation lies before you for a new covenant of Christian faith. Amen.

7

Humility and Exaltation: The Twenty First Sunday after Pentecost[1]

Joel 2:21–32; 2 Timothy 4:1–8, 11–18; Luke 18:1–14

Jesus said, "all who exalt themselves will be humbled, but all who humble themselves will be exalted." No principle is more central to the Christian Way than this. Matthew, Mark, and Luke cite Jesus saying that the first will be last and the last first. The Beatitudes bless the meek and say they shall inherit the earth. The most radical claim of Christianity, beyond any doctrines of cosmic sin and salvation, death and resurrection, or even of Jesus as judge and redeemer, is that the world's values are turned upside down. Those who are winners by worldly standards are in fact the losers if they are exalted and not humble. Those who are the losers by worldly standards are in fact the winners if they are humble and do not seek worldly exaltation. Not only was this a powerful, radical teaching in the early church, it was the point of the narrative of Jesus Christ himself. Saint Paul put it in the most dramatic way in the second chapter of his letter to the Philippians:

> Let the same mind be in you that was in Christ Jesus, who, though he was in the form of God, did not regard equality with God as something to be exploited, but emptied himself, taking the form of a slave, being born in human likeness. And being found in human

1. Preached October 24, 2004, the twenty-first Sunday after Pentecost.

form, he humbled himself and became obedient to the point of death—even death on a cross. Therefore God also highly exalted him and gave him the name that is above every name. (Phil. 2: 1–9)

Jesus humbled himself before poor, ignorant, corrupt, and oppressive human beings, and thus was exalted by God as Lord over all. Jesus was humble to the point of humiliation on the cross—what could be more humiliating than to be tortured to death as a common criminal, naked, in front of your mother and friends? Yet out of such humility comes new life and a proper exaltation before God. Without humility, our old sins keep us captive and we seek exaltation like the self-righteous Pharisee in Jesus's parable. With humility, no matter how sinful we are, like the tax collector, God forgives sins and exalts us like the risen Christ.

As a principle of ethics, humility is a virtue common to nearly all religions and humanistic traditions. The opposite of humility is something like arrogance, and arrogance is commonly thought to be a vice. In Jesus's teaching, however, the opposite of humility is not exactly arrogance but specious exaltation, the chief example of which is thinking oneself to be righteous in comparison with others and expecting others to recognize this superiority. In other teachings, being humble is quite compatible with being exalted. After all, some people are more righteous than others, and the educated righteous people know this. They construe themselves to be better, and often are recognized by others as being better, aristocrats of virtue. Good people are often exalted to positions of high power and responsibility. Surely we would not want unrighteous people in those positions. Exaltation to such positions with proper recognition and a proper self-consciousness about one's virtues is usually though to be quite compatible with humility. In fact, only the humble ought to be exalted to worldly power and recognition.

Yet Jesus took a slightly different approach. He was not against rich or powerful people; he was not against those who had gained the world's respect. But he was against people thinking that they are better than other people and accepting that self-exaltation. We should "judge not, that we be not judged," as he said in the Sermon on the Mount. Instead of thinking that we are better than others, even when that is palpably true, we should address the Almighty saying, "God, be merciful to me, a sinner!" If we repeat that mantra a hundred times a day—God, be merciful to me, a sinner!—everything in our ethical life will be different. We will be humble, and not touched by any circumstance of exaltation. And we will come to see people, not for their accomplishments, honors, riches, or exalted reputations, but for their humble practice, or lack thereof. Christians exalt the humble precisely because of their humility, not because of their righteousness, power, or wealth.

The principle of humility extends beyond the sphere of personal ethics to politics, I fear. Does a nation believe itself to be especially righteous in comparison with others, labeling them evil? Some nations surely are better than others, but all are sinful. Saddam Hussein was outrageous to invade Kuwait in order to control its oil. But was that motive lacking in the American invasion of Iraq? Saddam Hussein jailed people illegally and resorted to torture. But the American prisons in Iraq have held people secretly without account and the prisons in Guantanamo are filled with people taken while defending their country and religion, and held without due process. The exposure of torture and humiliation at Abu Graib shows, not that a few people misbehaved, but that such treatment is not uncommon in prisons in America whose jailers were hired for Iraq. How can America rail at some "axis of evil" when it should be saying, "God, be merciful to us, a sinful nation"?

The danger of political self-righteousness, especially when we know that America is not as bad as some other nations, is that it emboldens our nation to think it can simply do what it wants to impose its righteous will on the world. To be sure, democracy is the best form of government that we know, and the world would be a better place if it were thoroughly democratic. Yet to impose democracy on a people whose social forms are not fit for it is not itself democratic behavior: it is imperial tyranny. Democracy by definition comes from the self-assertion of the people. How can a nation invade others to impose democracy when its own voting machines don't work, many of its people are illegitimately disenfranchised, and lawsuits are threatened about election fraud before the election takes place? The humility of democracy means we should say, "God, be merciful to us, a sinful nation."

A nation moves from self-exaltation to plain arrogance when it asserts and exercises a right to make war on others simply because it has the power to do so and war serves its best interests for power and economic control. Where is the sense of moral limits to the exercise of violent power? When the Soviet Union was powerful, each super-power limited the other. With the demise of the Soviet Union some of our American neoconservative thinkers have argued that, in our current "unipolar" political situation, what is needed is a benevolent American empire. I commend to you a new book by the historian Gary Dorrien, called *Imperial Designs,* which traces the development of this neoconservative political philosophy. That no other nation wants a global American empire, though many want American protection and handouts, suggests more than a little self-exaltation and even arrogance in the neoconservative proposal. Given the world's problems of poverty, lack of education, the sleazy theft of wealth by national leaders, and violent clashes among cultures in multicultural societies, who would want imperial power in the hands of a nation whose economic policies widen the gap between its very poor and very rich, whose primary and secondary school systems lag behind those of many other developed nations, whose big businesses associated with governmental leaders are rocked by scandals, and whose government courts the favor of cultural groups that insist their values regarding life, death, sex, and domestic issues be imposed on the rest? America is not Zimbabwe or the Sudan by any means, cesspools of corruption. Neither is it the kingdom of God, as people must think who want to impose some version of the American way of life on other nations by force.

Only when America can present itself, saying, "God, be merciful to us, a sinful nation," can it legitimately exercise leadership to stimulate other nations to struggle against poverty, ignorance, corruption in government, and the oppression of other cultures by the most powerful culture. The world does not need to hear from America a hypocritical self-exalting righteousness backed by overwhelming force. It needs to hear that, though we have the power to sin outrageously, instead we restrain ourselves, humbly seek mercy for sins we acknowledge, and turn our power to amending our ways. The world needs to see America as a model of humble continuing self-transformation. Then it can request American help for transformation in other places of poverty, ignorance, corruption, and oppression, with each nation taking responsibility for its own democratic self-affirmation.

None of this is to suggest that the United States should let itself become militarily weak so as to be unable to defend itself when attacked or fulfill its defense treaty obligations to other nations. The international rings of criminal terrorists are an astonishing threat to civilized societies, and America needs to take the lead in international cooperation in gathering intelligence and effective police work. The Christian point about humility is that we should never use military or police force in a spirit of arrogance or self-exaltation, only and always in a spirit of humility that says first, "God, be merciful to us, a sinful nation."

We should remember that the American government is a secular enterprise in which Christian voices are mixed with many other constituencies. Moreover, not all Christian voices seem to heed Jesus's remark that "all who exalt themselves will be humbled, but all who humble themselves will be exalted." Many Christians seem instead to support the self-exaltation of a policy of imperial manifest destiny for America. Nevertheless, the gospel in its many statements is clear that the worldly values of exaltation are turned upside down in the kingdom of heaven and that humility is the only value worth exalting. Christians should promote humility in public life.

Humility, of course, begins with us individually and in our interpersonal relations. It is no simple virtue to learn. Self-exaltation easily disguises itself in forms of false humility, and we need to discern the counterfeits. We need to learn humility when we are powerful and wealthy with many kinds of resources. We need to learn humility when we are in fact among the elites in scientific, intellectual, and professional attainments, an especially poignant point for a congregation at a university church. The beginning of humility is a consciousness of faults that we present constantly to God, saying, "God, be merciful to me, a sinner." To keep ever before our minds the honest need for God's mercy is a good start to the work of exercising power and attainments with humility, a work that falls to each of us particularly and to Americans generally in this time.

So I invite you to see the world through Jesus's eyes. Those who exalt themselves saying, "God, I thank you that I am not like other people: thieves, rogues, adulterers, or even like this tax collector," are yet to be humbled. Those who come to God with downcast eyes and say, "God, be merciful to me, a sinner!" are justified before the merciful God and will have true exaltation. Amen.

8

Conversion[1]

Habakkuk 1:1–4; 2:1–4; 2 Thessalonians 1:1–4, 11–12; Luke 19:1–10

This is a day of many special observances. The text from Habakkuk begins, "O LORD, how long . . ."; those of you who are here have obviously mastered the transition from daylight saving to standard time. Habakkuk goes on to say that the political and moral situation of his nation is a disaster, but he holds out hope for a vision of a new time; today is the last Sunday before the elections, and more religious fervor has been poured out on this campaign than any in my rather long memory. Some people believe that the affairs of the Red Sox are more important than those of the election, but I dare not comment on that: freedom of speech in Boston does not go that far. The text from 2 Thessalonians is a grand expression of gratitude on Saint Paul's part for the steady increase in saintliness of his little flock in Thessaloniki. Today is the eve of All Saints' Day when we remember the saints who have died in the Lord. The secular celebration of Halloween these days seems to have come untethered from the religious holiday, but here in chapel we note the great cloud of witnesses with whom we live in eternity. Finally, to conclude the many special occasions of this day, Protestant churches commemorate the Reformation. Our Chapel Choir and

---

1. Preached October 31st, the twenty-second Sunday after Pentecost, Reformation Sunday, the Eve of All Saints' Day.

Collegium will perform Bach's marvelous Reformation cantata, "Ein Feste Burg."

I am going to pass for the moment on all these topics, however, to focus on the point of the gospel lesson, the power of Jesus to convert such a person as Zacchaeus. Religious conversion is an extremely contentious topic these days. American society is based on principles of religious tolerance, which usually means that we should treat people as fine just as they are, in terms of religion. Yet every religion believes that its own way is particularly apt for living out our destiny in relation to what is ultimate. Some religions, such as Advaita Vedanta and Judaism, tend to tie the aptness of their religion to a particular people, a social class, or ethnic group. Others, such as Buddhism, Christianity, and Islam, believe their way is apt for everyone, although they recognize historical associations with national and ethnic cultures.

In recent years we have seen the rise of fundamentalisms in nearly every religion, fundamentalisms that go beyond advocating their own path to attack the alternative paths as hopeless with regard to authenticity and salvation. Theologians call this strain of fundamentalism "exclusivism," the conviction that only one's own way is apt for the ultimate matters of life. Whereas the dark side of fundamentalism is a militant defensiveness and antagonism toward other ways of life, the bright side is a joyous compulsion to convert the others to one's own path for the sake of their own good. Nearly all religions accept converts who choose to join them and become worthy of acceptance. For theological exclusivists, conversion of others goes beyond offering them a choice that they can freely accept. For exclusivists, the obligation to convert others is part of loving them. Not to do everything possible to convert the others is like dismissing them as unimportant human beings.

Let me illustrate this with our situation here at the University. We have a complex chaplaincy that aims to serve the religious needs of all our students. Student groups representing a vast array of world religions are recognized and supported with regard to their leadership, facilities, and activities, all with the aim of fostering religious practices and maturity as befits university people. This emphasis on flourishing religious pluralism and tolerance flows directly from the theology of Methodism in the original School of Theology, which in turn founded Boston University. The first president of the University, William Fairfield Warren, was a professor of comparative religions as well as dean of the School of Theology. The rule at the University from the beginning has been that all people are to be supported in the practice of their religion and that no one is to be made to feel inferior because of their religion. This rule did not derive at Boston University from some secular Enlightenment principle of privatizing religion so that it does not count; it comes rather from the theological conviction that God's grace cannot be limited to any one path and that all may count.

The negative rule following from this has been and still is that proselytizing is forbidden on campus: you can explain your faith and invite others to join, but you cannot put pressure on them to do so. The University Chaplains work hard and cooperatively to encourage the religious practice of all the religious groups while at the same time preventing activities that seem to harass or disrespect people of other religions or no religion. Fine and delicate lines need to be drawn here separating the vigorous witness of a religion from the pressure to make others feel inferior, disrespected, or damned if they do not join it. All theological points can be debated, of course, in academic ways proper to university life. This happens frequently in informal conversation as well as formal discussions in classrooms and special events. But theological debates should not be framed in ways that target people for conversion. Respect for the others' beginning point is the precondition for intellectual debate in the civil society of the University.

You can imagine how difficult this rule against proselytizing is for students from exclusivistic religions. Converting others is close to the center of their intrinsic religious practice, and this because of imperatives to love and care. Yet they cannot do this here in ways that make the others feel pressured or harassed. Proselytizing is as much in the eye of the proselytized as it is in the intent of the proselytizer. Insistence on foundational respect as the principle of civil society in the University is hard on the evangelical Christians and fundamentalist Muslims who believe that others miss salvation. It is hard on observant Jews who have to be careful not to suggest that secular Jews are inferior as Jews because they are nonobservant. In cases like these, genuine religious conviction legitimately can be expressed only in ways that do not seem to be pressured existential criticisms of those who do not share them. The University Chaplains work very hard to help draw the proper lines.

Imperfect as our University system is for insisting on the foundational respect necessary for freedom of religion, would it not be a vast step toward world peace if all the world followed such a policy? Instead of such political idealism today, however, I commend to you Jesus's approach to converting

Zacchaeus. Note that Jesus did not attempt to convert Zacchaeus from one religion to another. Zacchaeus, like Jesus, was a Jew, a "son of Abraham," as Jesus put it. But Zacchaeus was a failure as a Jew. As a chief tax collector, he worked for the Roman occupation force. Tax collecting in those days was something like a franchise operation: the collector contracted with the government to raise a certain amount of money, and sometimes collectors were unscrupulous about how that was done. So Zacchaeus was a cheat, and he had made himself very wealthy at least in part by defrauding others. He admitted as much. All this was very contrary to even ordinary faithful Jewish practice, not to speak of the religious virtuosity of saintly Jewish people. The technical term for this kind of religious failure is that Zacchaeus was a "schlub." Every religion has schlubs, usually far more schlubs than saints and spiritual virtuosi.

Despite being a schlub, Zacchaeus longed for something he knew not what. He was so intrigued to see who Jesus was that he climbed a tree to get a better view; imagine a short, rich, chief governmental official doing something like that. What did Jesus do? He called him down from the tree, treated him respectfully, and said he would take Zacchaeus's hospitality. Apparently no one had treated Zacchaeus like that in a long time, because the effect was astonishing. People began to mutter against Jesus for associating with the likes of Zacchaeus, but Zacchaeus right there said he would give half his wealth to the poor, instantly becoming a virtuoso of charity. Right there he said he would pay back four times the amount he might have defrauded people. That not only was a confession of guilt and repentance but a saintly work to make amends: the Torah specified returning what you stole plus 20 percent, not 300 percent. Jesus said Zacchaeus had been lost, but that salvation had come to his house. That is true conversion, from being lost to being saved within the religion of his house, in this case as a son of Abraham like Jesus.

By no means do I want to minimize differences between religions. Disputing theological differences is my business as a professor. Nevertheless, the existential matters of faith have more to do with the difference between schlubs and saints than they do with differences between religious affiliations and theologies. I have taken part in many interreligious dialogues, with the universal experience that the leaders of the various faiths who engage one another have more in common with one another, and more mutual respect, than they do with the schlubs in their own religion. As a Protestant I agree with Luther's criticism of selling indulgences that would buy people a place in heaven, and with his insistence that each individual can be related directly to God, as well as indirectly through the church. So I guess the Reformation movement was preferable to the Roman Catholic establishment of its time. But I regret the vicious divisions it caused with all their wars, and I regret the action of Pope Leo X to excommunicate Lutherans, causing a still permanent schism. I have much more solidarity with and respect for saintly Catholics than I do with Protestant schlubs. No sectarian principle can limit God's grace to bring people to attention in ultimate matters. Why waste time trying to convert the saints of other religions when the fields are white with lost souls like Zacchaeus for whom many hands are needed for the harvest?

With regard to celebrating Reformation Day, let us do so with studied ambivalence, remembering that in Luther's great hymn, "A Mighty Fortress Is Our God," the enemy is Satan, not Catholics. With regard to celebrating All Saints' Eve, let us lift our hearts in joy for all the saints who attend on God, not only those of our fold. With regard to Habakkuk's hope for mitigating political disaster, let us remember that it is rich and powerful schlubs like Zacchaeus whose greed and corruption bring it on. With regard to the time, the time is now for us to catch the attention of the greedy and corrupt and bring them to a conversion like Zacchaeus's. The world is such a disaster now that the need for genuine conversion, after the model of Jesus, has ultimate urgency. May God be with us this week. Amen.

9

The Heavens, the Earth, the Sea, and the Dry Land[1]

Haggai 1:15b—2:9; Psalm 145;
Second Thessalonians 2: 1–5, 11–17; Luke 20:21–38

Most of you know the famous recitative from Handel's *Messiah* that precedes the Refiner's Fire aria. The standard English text is, "Thus saith the Lord, the Lord of Hosts: Yet once, a little while, and I will shake the heavens and the earth, the sea and the dry land, and I will shake, and I will shake all nations; I'll shake the heavens, the earth, the sea, the dry land, all nations, I'll shake; and the desire of all nations shall come. The Lord, whom ye seek, shall suddenly come to His temple; ev'n the messenger of the Covenant, whom ye delight in: behold, He shall come, saith the Lord of Hosts." This is our reading from Haggai in a slightly different translation. Haggai was a prophet when Cyrus of Persia returned the Jewish leadership to Jerusalem from exile in Babylon, and he was anxious to promote the rebuilding of the temple that had been destroyed a half century earlier. Haggai did not say, with Handel, that the Lord whom ye seek will come to the Temple; he said rather that the gold of all nations shall come to adorn the temple. Haggai was confident that the rebuilding of the temple would in fact rebuild the nation of Israel.

---

1. Preached November 7, 2004, the twenty-third Sunday after Pentecost.

My concern here is not with Haggai's building program but with God's power to shake. Of course, to say that God shakes the heavens, the earth, the seas, the dry lands, and all nations, is symbolic speech. God is the creator of the entire cosmos, including things that shake and are shaken. It cannot be true in a literal sense that God acts as a shaking agent within nature or nations. Symbolically, however, God's shaking of the most stable and steady parts of our world describes God's temporal creative Spirit. From our temporal historical standpoint, we can see God's Spirit as the creative force that builds things up and shakes them down. When we look toward the building up of things, we see God creating harmonies out of natural and social processes. Those processes on their own might never connect, they might inhibit one another, or even destroy one another. Divine creativity builds things up as it brings the processes into harmony. So in the ancient cosmology of the Bible, God creates the world by distinguishing within the original chaos between the heavens above and the earth beneath, between the surrounding seas and the dry land. Much of the story of the Hebrew Bible has to do with God creating a reasonably harmonious nation out of the rag-tag tribes of Israel. Psalm 139 says God knits things together in the mother's womb to create a person. So also in our own lives, we look to the divine Spirit to be creative in organizing the multitude of factors of our existence to gain an education, to raise a family, to work out a career. We look to the Spirit to bring justice to the relations among people and peace to the nations, all matters of organizing disharmonies into harmonies.

In Christian theology, the conditions for harmony as such are called the Logos, the Divine Word that is the universal precondition of all actual structures. John's Gospel says the Logos became incarnate in Jesus, so that Jesus harmonizes his path in the ideal way for human beings and also effects the harmonization of alienated people with God and each other. The harmonizing mode of the Divine Spirit leads to the achievement of the harmonies of existence.

The flip side is that the Spirit also has a dis-harmonizing mode, a destructive mode. Because we live in time, no harmony lasts forever. Every structure wears out. As scientists know, the energy required to maintain a specific kind of order when the conditions for sustaining that order no longer obtain is enormous—entropy means that all the achieved harmonies of the world will pass away as the energy is used up. If our careers do not adapt to new conditions, finding new energy, they fall apart. If our families don't continually reform, their static relations become prisons. Every human body wears out with age. Nations that cohere well at one time self-destruct as time passes if they do not reform to find new energy. A social structure that seems an advance in justice when it is established can become a scaffold of oppression. The very conditions that make for peace one year make for war the next.

Haggai made his point in reference to the most stable things in his universe: the heavens, the earth, the seas, and the dry land. God shall shake even them. The Divine Spirit in its destructive mode is as profound and thorough as the Divine Spirit in its harmonizing mode. Although it seems uncomfortable for Christians, who sometimes like to think of God as a well-intentioned manager of our universe who preserves all good things, we would do well to borrow the symbol of God the Destroyer from Hinduism, for that is what Haggai is getting at.

To be sure, we would like to think that destruction is for the sake of new and better harmonies. You need to break eggs to make a cake, the cliché goes, with the supposition that a cake is better than unbroken eggs Let us pray that the destruction, pain, decay, and collapses in our world go to serve some better, improved situation in the future.

But we should not kid ourselves that the gospel promises a better tomorrow out of the destructions of today. It promises only that each of us, our communities, and our nation, will be held accountable in ultimate perspective for who we are before God. It promises God's mercy and forgiveness. It promises a resurrected life with God. But it does not promise worldly success or a rosy future that somehow justifies the Spirit in the destructive mode with the Spirit in the harmonizing mode. Things just might get worse. For long periods of history, decline has been the main story rather than enhanced civilization. Hope lies in the bosom of God, not necessarily in success for tomorrow, although we do need to give our all, heart, mind, soul, and strength, to promoting justice and satisfaction in our time and to improving the future.

Another level of meaning of the Divine Spirit as the Shaker of the most apparently permanent things of the cosmos is that we must look to that Spirit in order to grieve loss. We need to rest awhile to witness and lament the destruction of things that have been good and important. Sometimes Christians want quickly to get past loss to new and better things. Many Christians like to jump from the crucifixion on Good Friday directly to the Resurrection on Easter Sunday. As my colleague in the School of Theology, Professor Shelly Rambo, says, this is to forget the hell of Holy Saturday when the death of the Logos can still be smelled, when God is gone on a distant Sabbath, and when nothing new has come to be. The Holy Spirit unifies its destructive and harmonizing modes in the remembrance, grief, and lament of the time between death and resurrection.

For many people in this nation the election this week was an extraordinary destruction of a treasured national identity that often has had the strength to risk its own prosperity and power in order to lead other nations to self-determination and prosperity of their own. The recent imperial adventures to force other nations to our will might have been an aberration of the electoral college four years ago. Now that program has been chosen by a majority, however slim. We have chosen to commit to "holding the course" rather than to learn new information and respond accordingly. We have chosen to get our way by our own military power rather than to trust allies who would help develop a reasoned common way. We have chosen religious values of simplistic certainty over faith in the grace to handle ambiguity and uncertainty. We have chosen a moral culture that reduces the color of life to black and white and seeks to impose the particulars of that vision on other cultures. These choices destroy forever America's innocent confidence in its own virtue, even while they attempt to justify themselves by that false righteousness. We are now as dangerous to the rest of the world and to our own people as any nation on earth, and by deliberate majority choice.

We Christians, of course, operate in the world as humble peacemakers, attempting to heal and bring about reconciliation. At least some Christians take this as their calling. This fellowship of reconciliation has a natural course when our people are agreed in distant essentials and differ over proximate strategies. But reconciliation is filled with wrenching ironies when the common essentials are lost and Christians are forced into opposition to their fellows, not mere difference. I fear we have lost the common essentials and, in order to bear true Christian witness, need to go into opposition to the majority culture, which includes many who also name themselves Christians.

God has shaken the heavens and the earth, the seas and the dry lands, and all nations. We need to seek out the Holy Spirit to understand and grieve the good that has been lost, and also to understand and commit ourselves to any new good that witnesses to what we can best understand as Christian righteousness, piety, faith, hope, and love. Although we are comfortable with the Holy Spirit in the harmonizing mode, we must grit our teeth to seek out the Holy Spirit in the destructive mode. Now is the time to do that, to sit with grief and uncertainty and find God in precisely that. Of course, many people look at the election as a victory rather than a source of grief. For them the Holy Spirit in the harmonizing mode is quite enough. But for those who grieve, the Holy Spirit who comes destroying and confusing is the source of strength while we wait for orientation to what's next. The Holy Spirit in both modes is present at the eucharistic table where we eat the symbols of torture and death while joined in a body that metabolizes death to new life. The Way of that body is to bear, believe, hope, and endure all things. I invite you to join this body at the table that has borne far greater losses and confusions than we endure at this time. Amen.

10

Endurance[1]

Isaiah 65:11–25; 2 Thessalonians 3:1–13; Luke 21:1–19

The lectionary gives us three amazing readings today. The text from Isaiah comes from the time that the Jews exiled in Babylon were being sent back to rebuild Jerusalem and its temple. Its song of hope stirs our hearts even today: a new heaven and a new earth. Remember last week's prophetic text from Haggai that said that God will shake the heavens and the earth. For Isaiah, the new Jerusalem will be a joy: no weeping will be there, no children will die in infancy, death at a hundred years will be considered premature, people will build and plant and enjoy the fruit of their labor. God will answer prayers as they are prayed, the wolf and the lamb shall feed together, the lion shall eat straw like the ox, the evil serpent will eat dirt, and "They shall not hurt or destroy on all my holy mountain, says the LORD."

Don't we need to hear such a word of hope in our time? Instead of peace we have war; instead of prosperity we have unbridled greed that besots the rich and beggars the poor; instead of glorying in nature's harmony, we destroy it for gain; instead of a harmonious world order, the civilization of the West is set against the civilization of Islam. The world's most powerful nation has made itself a loadstone for terrorists where no one is secure, and has so mortgaged its future that others will reap what it plants. We need

---

1. Preached November 14, 2004, the twenty-fourth Sunday after Pentecost.

to hear that there will be a new heaven and a new earth, and that our temple will be restored.

The Jerusalem of which Isaiah spoke was indeed restored and a new temple built grander than the old one. That new temple was precisely the one Jesus predicted would be destroyed, with not one stone left on another. Jerusalem, and Israel as a nation, would be destroyed too. All that happened in fact between Jesus's time and the time Luke wrote his gospel. Isaiah's new heaven and new earth lasted only about 550 years, and even during much of that time Israel was an occupied country.

Jesus also said that his followers were in for a hard time. If they were to remain true in their witness to his gospel, they would be arrested and persecuted, betrayed even by their family and friends. Moreover, they would be called to testify to their neighbors and in public life before high governmental figures. They would be put in prison and subjected to the authority of religion hostile to Jesus's true gospel. All these things did indeed happen between the time of Jesus and the time Luke wrote his gospel—many of them are recorded in Luke's second volume, the Acts of the Apostles.

Our situation is more like the one Jesus was talking about than Isaiah's. Because it is so difficult, and Jesus's followers would be roundly hated and some put to death, he said that they would save their souls by their endurance. He did not say they would escape persecution and death, but through endurance while they lived, they would escape the loss of their souls, a theme he talked about quite a lot. Paul put the point even more directly: to endure in a time of perilous Christian witness people have to work hard. If anyone in the community of witnesses will not work, let them not eat!

Now how does all this apply to us? I need to begin with a little personal testimony. I came to adolescent political consciousness after the Second World War, which I thought on the whole was a just war, won by the right side. I took pride in the United Nations as a positive if imperfect step toward democracy and the containment of violence. The Cold War was scary, but it turned out that no one really wanted war and Communism's totalitarianism was simply not viable. I grew up in the civil rights movement, which recognized a great and long-standing evil and actually made significant progress to rectify it. Of course the brutal effects of slavery have not been erased, but they are tractable to progress, I thought. The Vietnam War, and the countercultural revolution it spawned, seemed to me the painful ending of the era of Western imperialism. I hoped that the hippie movement would mature into a humbler conception of the role of America in the world and an economic worldview that would set stringent controls on the evil excesses of capitalism, while acknowledging its obvious benefits as an economic system. Although the culture of consumerism had long been recognized as a demonic parody of the culture of freedom, the very fact that this had long been recognized and criticized meant to me that it was not out of control. In sum, as I matured as a Christian I thought that the Christian critique of American culture was in place, and that I could participate in applying its pressures to the social, cultural, and political scenes of my time. In fact, I thought that the Christian critique of American culture was itself a powerful part of that very culture.

The recent election, however, has disabused me of that view, which I think was shared by many. I believe now that the choices made in the election render a serious Christian witness dangerous, as it has been at so many points in history, and for that very reason all the more necessary. I believe the Christian witness will divide families as it has rarely done in recent history. It will be punished by a government that treats disagreement as unpatriotic and unsupportive of our soldiers who occupy foreign countries. The religious culture that has recently achieved establishment status by its contribution to the election will condemn Christian witness as heretical to its alternate vision of what that witness is. Because there is such disagreement as to what that witness is, permit me to say what I think its basic tenets are.

First, in the arena of international politics the Christian witness is primarily to peacemaking. After 9/11 it was of course imperative for the American people and government to support a vigorous international police action to apprehend the murderous terrorists and break up the terrorist rings around the world that threaten everyone's security. But even more imperative for Christian witness, the American people and government should have taken preemptive action to make sure there were no warlike responses and to investigate the reasons and conditions for the 9/11 attack. When people are so aggrieved as to resort to widely supported terrorism, their grievances need to be addressed at the front of our agenda. Christian liberals are called weak because they want to eliminate the anger that fuels terrorism, yet that is the Christian witness to peacemaking. Because our nation has consistently chosen war over peacemaking on this issue, our witness needs continually to criticize that choice and devise steps toward peacemaking now.

Second, although justice is always important, a dimension of every Christian critical endeavor, the Christian witness is that judgment should be left to God and that Christian effort should be to help the poor and relatively powerless. While our nation has vaunted its strength and wealth, it has also let the poor get poorer at home on many fronts, for instance in jobs, education, welfare, taxation, and community participation. The Christian witness should always be in solidarity with the poor, and if that looks like weakness to the rich and powerful, so be it.

Third, Christian witness needs always to lead from a position of humility rather than arrogance and self-righteousness. The very idea that America should insist that its own righteousness justifies masking motives for war with lies so easily found out, disregarding the interests and advice of allies, and claiming that anyone who criticizes the government is unpatriotic and helpful to the "enemy," is abhorrent to Christian witness. If Jesus could say, in reference to himself, that no one is good except God, how can the government claim such goodness and represent itself as religious?

Fourth, the Christian witness should be to a generous acceptance of all peoples and their religions, with the same critical tools brought to Christian theology as should be brought to the theologies of others. Jesus represented this in his inclusive table fellowship and in his courteous treatment of people from other religions (Samaritans, Canaanites, and pagan Romans). Jesus said he had sheep of other folds than that of his own disciples. His God would create no people who are not loved and filled with grace in spiritual as well as other matters. Christian witness needs to be sounded loud and clear against bigotry and exclusivism, even when that seems to be a liberal pampering of enemies. Christians should tolerate no one to remain their enemy if it is at all possible to change that.

Fifth, the Christian witness should always be to love. "Love your enemies," said Jesus. Love is perhaps too personal a trait to be a political virtue. Yet love or its lack is the inner formation of the attitudes that shape public policies. Christian witness needs to expose the hate that demonizes gays and lesbians, African Americans, and women who seem too uppity, Jews who insist on not being Christians, Muslims who think Americans are greedy, and liberals who put principle above patriotism. The other side of exposing hate is reaching out to the haters in love.

Sixth, the Christian witness should always be to courage over fear. Christians are confident of the salvation that comes from God and have no need to fear what the world brings, however canny and prudent we should be. People with no real God strike out in fear against real, imagined, and demonized enemies. They let fear keep them from peacemaking, helping the poor, taking the humble place, the acceptance of people who are different from themselves, and the risks of love. Fear makes them warmongers, greedy for themselves, arrogant as a form of whistling in the dark, bigots, and haters. Such fear is incompatible with the Christian faith, which says that "neither death, nor life, nor angels, nor rulers, nor things present, nor things to come, nor powers, nor height, nor depth, nor anything else in all creation, will be able to separate us from the love of God in Christ Jesus our Lord." Most of all, courage is the Christian witness against the fear of ambiguity and confusion. Christian faith accepts life's ambiguities and witnesses to the power of God's grace to get us through.

Seventh, and most important for people whose religious connection is with a university church, the Christian witness is to the complexity of life before God. To understand the complexities of life, including its ambiguities, requires dedicated, sophisticated, complex thinking, which is a primary way of worshiping the divine Word. The Christian witness to this is both negative and positive. Negatively, the Christian witness needs to expose and ridicule simplistic religion and simplistic politics. The worst kind of theology is that which reduces itself to a simple story with winners and losers, God's people and the enemy. Theology of that sort sells a lot of books these days, and it should be exposed for the satanic simplification that it is. Positively, Christian witness needs to enter into the kind of complex inquiry that can sort through complicated issues and deal with ambiguities. Political and economic issues are difficult enough, and Christian witness should support scholars inquiring about them. Theological issues are even more complicated, and Christian witness should demand preaching and teaching equal to the task. Set aside the desire for a simple take-home message and demand to be shown the complex insides of issues. Christian thinking needs to respect the witness of peacemaking, solidarity with the poor, humility, neighborliness, love, and courage. Yet that respect should never lead it to simplifications that lie.

Peacemaking, solidarity with the poor, humility, neighborliness across cultures, love, and courageous confidence in God's grace, are not the exclusive preserve of the Christian witness. Change the rhetoric only slightly and those points can be the witnesses of Jews and Muslims, Buddhists and Hindus, Daoists and Confucians. They all point to a counterculture against the recent majority. The unanimity of that ecumenical religious witness gives great hope in a time when all need to go into opposition to the majority culture, however slim the majority is. The most important power of witness is that it can bring light to those who had mistaken martial strength, wealth, arrogance, prideful bigotry, self-righteous hatred, and defensive fear, for wisdom. The people who have made those mistakes are our fathers and mothers, brothers and sisters, children, and friends. Not for winning the next election, but for the sake of their souls, and ours, let us endure together to touch the Spirit and voice the witness of the Crucified and Risen One. Amen.

II

To Be Awake[1]

Isaiah 2:1–5; Romans 13:11–14; Matthew 24:36–44

If any of us were tempted to think of Advent, which begins today, as only a preliminary to Christmas, the feast of the incarnation of God in Jesus, our texts today would disabuse us. Advent is not preparation for the coming of Baby Jesus: it celebrates the *second* coming of Jesus in judgment. The theme of our texts is that we should wake up for that judgment and be ready. The theme for next week's texts is that we should repent in the face of impending judgment. The mood of Advent is urgency.

Because Advent and the Christmas incarnation repeat every year in the liturgical calendar, we know that they are not simply historical matters. The long-ago birth of Jesus was not significant only for its time. It has an eternal once-for-all significance that Christians need to reconsider and appropriate every year. The same with Advent: its significance is eternal and once for all. Because the imagery of the second coming seems to be in the historical future, the fact Jesus has not come for so long tempts many people to dismiss the message of judgment. If Advent referred only to a future event, the chances of it happening in our lifetime are so remote we can safely forget it. The urgency of Jesus's preaching about imminent judgment cannot be sustained very long if it means merely a future event.

Already in the New Testament writers such as John and the authors of Ephesians and Colossians were saying that judgment is less a future

---

1. Preached November 28, 2004, the first Sunday of Advent.

temporal event to be anticipated than an eternal state of affairs that is always relevant now. The theological term "realized eschatology" means that we are eternally before God, which means in part "judgment now." Realized eschatology is the opposite of literalist views of the second coming as a future event, made popular in our time by the Left Behind series of books. The literalist reading of Jesus's apocalyptic language, and that in other parts of the Bible, gives rise to some unexpected policies. For instance, many of our evangelical colleagues strongly support the State of Israel, not for the sake of Israel or Jews or out of respect for Jewish religion, but because they hope that enough Jews will convert to Christianity to trigger the second coming. That is actually an anti-Jewish policy. Sometimes literalist readers of apocalyptic biblical passages are in favor of war and chaos, a literal self-destruction of civilizations, also in hope that this will trigger the second coming. How far that is from the ethical injunctions to peacemaking that form the content of Jesus's particular judgment! The result of repeated non-appearances of Jesus, despite temporary excited expectations, is that people finally dismiss Jesus's apocalyptic language with a "ho-hum."

The real point of Jesus's message, I believe, is that we stand eternally before God and everywhere and always are under judgment, not later but now. The problem, Jesus said, is that we are like sleepwalkers and are unaware of this. We are like people before the flood, eating, drinking and marrying without knowing what is going on. Two people will be at work as if everything were normal and suddenly one dies. The householder sleeps on while the thief breaks in. The Gospel of Matthew is filled with parables about people being asleep or unaware of what is going on, such as the story of the tenants who thought they could kill the landowner's agents, even his son, and get away with it, or the story of the marriage feast where the poor guest did not know what occasion to dress for and was condemned to the outer darkness, or the story of the sleepy virgins who missed the bridegroom, or the remark about the people who can't tell from the buds on the fig tree that summer is coming. Jesus said, "Keep awake." "Be ready."

To apply Jesus's point generally to our lives does not take rocket science. We know how easy it is to become so immersed in the daily struggles of life that we forget life's real significance. Mundane things seem difficult enough that we don't have time for religious matters, except insofar as they can become our mundane routine. Of course we recognize that we have moral struggles, with selfishness, neglect of others, failure to be attentive to people's needs, and the rest. We know we need to do something about that, and we will, tomorrow. For today we have to get the term paper written, pay the bills, or get some relief from life's stresses. To this Jesus says, "Wake up," because tomorrow you might be dead. What you might do later to make amends is suddenly irrelevant. Jesus says, live before God as if you were ready to die. Part of the urgency of the Advent season is that this one might be our last.

Jesus had in mind something more specific than this point, however. When he thought of people standing before God in judgment, he understood that the ethics according to which they would be judged is that derived from the Torah and the Prophets. He liked to quote Isaiah, for instance, and our passage from the second chapter of Isaiah is particularly instructive. For Isaiah, the divine judgment was not so much God coming to judge individuals, as in Jesus's examples, as it was the glorious elevation of Jerusalem, God's city. Isaiah envisioned a future in which Jerusalem would be the capital of the world and all of the nations would come to it for judgment. The reason for nations to stream to Jerusalem, Israel's holy hill, would not be that Jerusalem has a particularly powerful or wise king. Rather it would be because God, not some human king, will instruct and judge the nations. "Many peoples shall come and say, / 'Come, let us go up to the mountain of the LORD, / to the house of the God of Jacob; / that he may teach us his ways / and that we may walk in his paths.' For out of Zion shall go forth instruction, and the word of the LORD from Jerusalem. // He shall judge between the nations, / and shall arbitrate for many peoples." Perhaps Isaiah was hoping that this would be the future of Jerusalem, which in his time was sore pressed by the Assyrians. The point for us is that nations lie under judgment, and given the choice would, or should, go to God for instruction and judgment. Isaiah's image of Zion as the place to stand before God is like Jesus's images of heaven, or the coming Son of Man.

The religious result of Isaiah's imagined encounter of all peoples with God on Mount Zion is like the heart of Jesus's teachings: "They shall beat their swords into plowshares, / and their spears into pruning-hooks, / nation shall not lift up sword against nation, / neither shall they learn war any more." Isaiah's prophetic song of divine-human encounter in the Lord's place was a song of peace. Jesus, the Prince of Peace, said, in the Beatitudes, that the peacemakers are the children of God. When Jesus said we would be judged, at the heart of his prophetic message was that we shall be judged as peacemakers.

To Be Awake

We've gone to sleep on that one, haven't we? Because the world has enough people ready to go to war when they think they can get away with it and advance their cause, Christians particularly ought to be peacemakers. Peacemaking is not only truce-making, a catch-up response after a war is started. Peacemaking is seeking out the frustrations, angers, and greed that give rise to war in the first place. How ironic it is, then, that the Western imperial nations sought to spread Christianity around the globe through their conquests but then failed to be awake to the peacemaking lesson of Christianity when their empires collapsed. The retreat of European and American imperialism from Africa, from the Muslim world stretching from Morocco to Indonesia, from India, Pakistan, Vietnam, the Philippines and Cuba, left a vast terrain of landmines ready to explode with slight provocation: ruinous divisions of the rich from the poor, puppet governments that did not care for their people, corrupt rulers and ruling families, national boundaries drawn without regard to cultures, and apartheid structures of one sort or another. India alone seems to have emerged stronger in its days of freedom than in its imperial days, and that is probably because its revolution was led by a pacifist peacemaker, Mahatma Ghandi; even India seems to have a perpetual war with Pakistan. Why were the so-called Christian imperial nations asleep to the ways their withdrawals set conditions for ongoing warfare? Why have Christians since then been asleep to what should be done to alleviate poverty and ignorance, stamp out corruption, and redistribute the world's wealth, so that the Third World doesn't need to look on the First World with envy and hate? Of course, Western imperialism is not responsible for every nation's ills, and many Christians indeed have acted as peacemakers—they are the heroes of our time. But the so-called Christian nations have been deep in slumber about the responsibilities of preventative peacemaking.

And what are we Christian Americans to say about our current situation? Granted, something needed to be done after 9/11, and it should have been aggressive, preemptive peacemaking. Instead, the government declared a war on terror and pumped up the inflated rhetoric of patriotic warmongering. The war on terror itself has been a bust because the terrorists just duck; the leaders are still at large and the rank and file is growing. The government has gone to war with Afghanistan and Iraq, however, two countries that did not attack us. Iraq had neither weapons of mass destruction nor any close connection with terrorism. Whatever our government's real motives were, disguised by its lies about terrorism and weapons of mass destruction, we are now engaged in continual wars from which it seems we cannot withdraw without causing even more damage. The Taliban are gaining in Afghanistan, and Fallujah was liberated by being destroyed, with the insurgents driven out to new hideouts. Now disaffected young men of the Muslim world are flocking to Iraq, a terrorist recruitment of our own making. The government seems to think that only more war can solve the problem. Meanwhile our poor soldiers occupying Iraq and Afghanistan are the targets of people whom they were misled to believe would welcome them, dying in a war that should never have been started.

How could Christians have been so soundly asleep as to support the government's policy of glorifying war and defining peace as only what can be sustained by the threat or use of violent force? We know that 71 to 80 percent of the regular churchgoing Christians voted to support that government. We are a church of sleepwalkers. Too many Christians have been hypnotized to believe that war is the road to peace. Too many have fallen asleep to the Christian witness to help the poor. Too many have slept through Jesus's lesson that humility, not arrogance, is the only way to lead. Too many have gone to sleep believing that only their own culture is worthy. Too many have been dulled by the narcotic of fear rather than awakened to the power of Christian courage. Too many have been anesthetized to complex, critical thinking by the sound bites of religious jingoism. Too many have translated the gospel into their parochial culture without remainder.

And now the Son of Man is calling us to account. "Wake up," he says. See what you are doing and remember the foundations of your faith, the gospel values for which Jesus died and to which the martyrs testified, the instructions of God on Zion. This Advent is for the sleeping Christians. It is not a season of comfort yet, but of urgency. Amen.

12

Repent[1]

Isaiah 11:1–10; Romans 15:1–13; Matthew 3:1–12

The main mission of John the Baptist, the hero of our gospel lesson, was to preach repentance, and then to baptize people as a sign of the seriousness of their return to virtue. Jesus came to John for baptism, and this was the occasion for John to point to Jesus as someone greater than himself. Christians since have transformed baptism into a once-for-all initiation rite rather than just a repentance rite. But we do celebrate the Eucharist as a repeatable rite that seals the bond of God with Jesus's people. A crucial preparation for the Eucharist is a prayer of confession, which we just recited together. Confession is a preliminary step in repentance.

The sharp point of the Baptist's remarks about repentance in our gospel text is what he says to the scribes and Pharisees, whom, with his customary good humor, he calls a "brood of vipers" and accuses of hypocrisy. He says that they ought to bear the fruit worthy of repentance, and that they don't. "Even now the axe is lying at the root of the trees; every tree therefore that does not bear good fruit is cut down and thrown into the fire." Confession of sin is not enough: we have to do something about it and mend our ways. Confession is admitting that we have gone in the wrong direction. Repentance is actually turning around and going the right way.

On this second Sunday of Advent, as we are about to gather around the Lord's table, we can ask whether we are a repentant people. As a nation

1. Preached December 5, 2004, the second Sunday of Advent.

we seem not to be peacemakers when we should be, not to care for the poor when that stands in the way of making the rich richer, not to exercise leadership from a position of humility. We seem to be defensive out of fear rather than kindly out of courage, self-assertive rather than loving, simplistic in our thinking rather than realistically complex, and convinced that one culture fits all and is above criticism. I recognize that other people interpret our national situation less gravely, and I hope they are right. But it seems to me that we do not bear the fruits of repenting pride in war, greed, arrogance, fear, national self-assertion over others, stereotyping, lies, and intolerance. Our nation has not turned back to Christian values in these matters, whatever else might justify our policies.

But not all of us favor the national course. Let me say no more about repentance for those who do favor our current national directions: the coalition of those who do is highly diverse, with many motives and differing cultural suppositions among themselves, as well as diverse understandings of the situation. I want to focus rather on what those have to repent who do not favor the national course, among whom I count myself. To be sure, each of us is highly inventive regarding sin, and we all have jillions of things to repent in particular. But my question is reaching for what went wrong among liberal Christians in America who now are so angry, grief-stricken, and depressed because we see our country to have become an aggressor nation when we thought it stood for justice and the protection of the weak, and we see our religion to have been defined publicly by a conservative version with which we share little but common symbols, interpreted very differently.

I have been struggling with this question, and have found a clue in some responses to the sermons I have been preaching recently. Several people have asked me, in one way or another, how they should relate to their conservative evangelical friends and relatives with whom they are in such fundamental and grievous disagreement, people they love despite the disagreements. Of course there is no pat answer to this, but the question itself is revealing. The culture wars in this country have been going on for decades, ever since the resurgence of fundamentalism in President Reagan's "moral majority." The theological religious disputes between conservatives and liberals have gone on for almost two centuries. What have we liberals been missing, or not doing, such that suddenly it seems like a new problem to relate in friendly Christian fashion to the Evangelical Right?

Repent

To be sure, part of it is that we have not been thinking that the Right could co-opt our country and the public face of our Christianity, and it has suddenly done so. This was simply false pride on the part of the religious moderates and liberals. But there is a deeper failure here in liberal Christianity. It has to do with what I call "the paradox of liberal tolerance." Whereas many outspoken conservative religious thinkers have no qualms about straightforwardly condemning liberal Christianity as unchristian and immoral, liberals have always insisted on tolerance of their opponents. Whereas our conservative sisters and brothers revel in sharp-edged issues such as Scripture first and last, liberals insist on taking into account every point of view. Whereas religious conservatives most often define morality by what they are against—abortion, stem cell research, and gay marriage in the recent debates—liberals define morality by large values to which they are committed, such as peacemaking, solidarity with the poor, humility, courage in the face of ambiguity, love, cultural diversity, acceptance of complexity, and so forth—all fuzzy values that find specific meaning only in complex application in ambiguous situations. For most liberals, sharp-edged absolute values without particular contexts are ideological fictions good for nothing but verbal warfare.

Three things result from this difference between religious conservatives and liberals. First, liberals tend to respond to conflict by moving to the middle in order to be accommodating, apparently abandoning their own principles. Second, liberals tend not to articulate their own positions for fear of exacerbating conflict. Third, liberals look mushy and spineless whereas the conservatives look like they stand for something, and by standing for something definite they can rally people to their cause.

What we liberals need to repent of, therefore, is the failure to distinguish the practical work of bringing about harmony and Christian reconciliation from the clarion delineation of the essential Christianity to which liberal Christians are committed. The latter, the call to the positive liberal Christian way of life, is the more important of the two, because it is the justification for the reconciliation with other forms of Christianity. Conservative evangelicals tend to view reconciliation and religious harmony as signs of weakness.

The fruit of repentance for liberal Christians, therefore, should be a vigorous statement of the Christian faith and definite programs that put it into practice. This means, I believe, at least seven things:

First, a fulsome theological elaboration of the great symbols and themes of the Christian belief in creation and redemption in Jesus Christ, without supernaturalism;

Second, a detailed reading of the Bible, without crippling authoritarianism or literalism, but informed by all we can know about reading the message of texts;

Third, a clear theology of the Christian community that does not insist that one culture be imposed on all but that articulates the obligations of many cultures living together with the norms of righteousness, piety, faith, hope, and love;

Fourth, definite and specific programs for influencing public life in ways that operationalize Christian values of peacemaking, solidarity with the poor, humility, the courage to risk love, restraint on power, cultural inclusiveness, complexity of thought, and all the rest;

Fifth, the development of specific demanding practices of spiritual discernment, formation, and growth that promote sanctification, without tying this to any one culture's manners;

Sixth, personal and institutional commitment to the most sophisticated and complex kinds of inquiry by which our world and God might be known, without the reduction of discourse to sound bites;

And seventh, the rigorous education of Christians in these theological and spiritual habits so that we can be conspicuous witnesses in public life, not embarrassed about the particularities of our faith but eloquent in testimony.

The fruits that distinguish liberal repentance in our time, in short, are clear theology without supernaturalism, biblical understanding without literalism or authoritarianism, church life without cultural imperialism, political life based on Christian values without cultural imperialism, demanding spiritual life without cultural imperialism, complex thinking without authoritarianism, and Christian witness without simplistic parochialism. Only when we repent of accommodation and timidity by pursuing these fruits of repentance with vigor can liberal Christians have the strength to reach out to our evangelical brothers and sisters who otherwise seem to us to have stolen our religion and country.

I invite you to come now to the table of the Lord with the confidence that your Christian convictions belong here. In fact they are needed as fruits of repentance for the failure to be proper witnesses to the faith. At this table you will find people of deep conviction who might disagree with you. At this table you will find people who are seeking their way through confusion and doubt. At this table you will find deeper expressions of your own Christian commitments. But I hope that at this table you will find very few people who don't care. Most of all, at this table you will find the God who comes to us this Advent and every moment, the God whose coming makes our responses to the issues of life matters of infinite urgency. As John the Baptist said, there is something better than and beyond the baptism of repentance, namely, the baptism of fire and the Holy Spirit, the fire of love, the Holy Spirit of reconciliation. Come, Lord Jesus. Come, People, to the table. Amen.

13

Inauspicious Beginnings[1]

Isaiah 63:1–9; Hebrews 2:11–18; Matthew 2:11–23

According to Luke, the angelic host sang to the shepherds, "Glory to God in the highest heaven, and on earth peace among those whom he favors." Christmas is the celebration of peace on earth, for it means that God is in our midst. The mystery of the incarnation is that God comes to us. We do not have to go to God: God comes to us.

In our reflective moments, of course, we smile at the fanciful stories surrounding the birth of Jesus, taking them with a grain of salt even as we love them. Even the logic of God "coming to us" is fancifully symbolic: God is our Creator and we are nothing without God. God cannot be apart from us at all, else we would not exist. So God cannot literally come to us from somewhere else. But we live in the dark about the foundations of our own existence so much of the time that the light that enlightens our true estate seems dimmed. The incarnation means that this true light has not been overcome by the darkness and in fact the light in Jesus calls this to our attention in saving ways. You recognize that I am paraphrasing John's Gospel's version of the Christmas story: "What has come into being in him [that is, Jesus] was life, and the life was the light of all people. The light shines in the darkness, and the darkness did not overcome it." (John 1:1–5)

The lesson the angels drew from the incarnation was peace. Because of Christmas, we have a very deep peace. But it is not a peace we can easily

---

1. Preached December 26, 2004, the first Sunday after Christmas.

understand. Of all the attributes that characterize our world civilizations today, peace seems not among them. So we need to look closely at what the biblical notion of peace in this sense might be.

The gospel lesson today reports the horror of Jesus's birth, not the pretty part. Herod the King was furious that a messiah might be born so he killed all of the children in the Bethlehem area under two years of age. Think of that! Our government calls the slaughter of innocents in the pursuit of one's goal "collateral damage." Fortunately, Jesus's family had been warned that something like this might happen, so they became refugees in Egypt, probably for about eight years. When they returned, Joseph was afraid to stay in Judea, where Bethlehem was, and settled north in Nazareth of Galilee, again a refugee. This was an inauspicious beginning for the incarnation and its strange peace.

Our passage from Isaiah praises God for all he has done for the house of Israel, showing them mercy according to the abundance of his steadfast love. In fact, Isaiah cites God saying of Israel, "Surely they are my people, / children who will not deal falsely"; and Isaiah says God will be their savior in all their distress. Isaiah goes on to say, after our reading, that the people were not faithful and that God did abandon them, only to try to claim them later. The house of Israel did not last, David's line was cut off, and after a lapse of nineteen centuries Israel today survives only by force of arms, not the active protection of God as alleged in the days of Moses. To generalize the point, the biblical promises of God to Israel have not been carried through, and we read these promissory texts as if they were the attempts of a beleaguered people to explain to themselves why they were special to God when history made them seem like minor players, even losers.

What do we make of the divine promises? Those of you who remember the liturgical greeting with which we began our Sunday worship during Advent know that we spoke approvingly of the "sure and certain promises of God" that came to fruition in Jesus, with a similar promise that Jesus would come again. Was that rhetorical overkill, or perhaps whistling in the dark? For, surely history has given the lie to those promises, unless you put up with indefinite postponement. Or perhaps the promises were not about history, as they seemed, but about something else. At any rate, whatever peace we have does not derive from any historical confirmation of divine promises.

Perhaps history is not the right arena in which to look for the incarnation or God's victory. Christianity in America today is divided into two main families of response to this issue. Many of our conservative brothers and sisters are convinced that the Bible is to be read very much as a commentary on history and a prophetic historical document. The kind of theology expressed in the Left Behind series of books is an extreme example, though highly persuasive to many people, of the theology that regards Christianity as a witness to a cosmic historical war between God and Satan. Historical events are taken to have supernatural meaning relative to this war, and biblical prophecies are taken to refer to coming historical but supernaturally significant events. Human beings on this view are not at all decisive actors in this war, but are rewarded according to whether they are loyal to God's side. One of the major battles of the war was when Jesus redeemed sinful humanity from the clutches of Satan, according to this interpretation. This historically oriented Christianity looks to the conversion of the Jews in Israel and the return of Christ for the last battle.

Biblical symbols for this conservative view of Christianity as literally historical come from the influences of Persian thought on Judaism during the Babylonian exile and subsequent Hellenistic culture. Portions of Isaiah, the book of Daniel, most of the authentic letters of Paul, and the book of Revelation can be read in support of this view, although they also can be read in other ways. Our text from Hebrews can be read this way when it says, "Since, therefore, the children share flesh and blood, he himself likewise shared the same things, [speaking of Jesus] so that through death he might destroy the one who has the power of death, that is the devil, and free those who all their lives were held in slavery by the fear of death." For Christians of the conservative historical persuasion, it is easy to believe that the enemies of Christian nations such as America are the Antichrist and that our wars have divine sanction as theologically righteous. Many conservative Muslims feel just the same way, though with the divinity on their side: the Iranian Muslim hate-word for the United States is the "Great Satan."

For many other Christians with more liberal theology, the ideals of peace and justice outweigh the goals of vindication in the prophetic texts, and the person and teachings of Jesus are far more important than Paul's account of the cosmic battle between supernatural forces. Liberal theologians emphasize the Gospels, as well as Ephesians, Colossians, James, and the Letters of John. For these Christians, the cosmos is understood in scientific terms, and the first-century image of cosmic supernatural battles is laid down to ancient but false speculations. History for many of these liberal

Christians does not have one unifying meaning as if it were a story, but rather is the arena in which social forces in different times and places interplay to produce crises of famine and plenty, justice and oppression, peace and war. Christian engagement is not merely to witness a war between supernatural agents but rather is to bring peace, justice, and abundance to the situations as they arise on our watch, precisely because Christ is with us. History as a whole does not have a narrative meaning. But history provides many contexts in which the meaning of human life is played out in communities and individuals according to the values of peace, justice, piety, faith, hope, and love, and in which human responsibility is very important, not mere witness.

During much of the course of Christianity these two theological approaches have coexisted, differing mainly in stress and emphasis. This was because both sides used to recognize that all language about God is symbolic and each could acknowledge the symbolic truth of the other side even if each thought its own side was more nearly literal. Now, however, fundamentalism has wrenched the conservative side to an uncompromising literalism. Liberal theology too, alas, has sometimes taken the alleged literalism of science to mean that symbolic thinking of any kind in theology has no standing regarding the truth. There seems to be little middle ground save in those churches with a rich symbolic liturgy that are willing to use the symbols in full knowledge that they cannot be taken literally. I myself stand in the middle ground with a theology of symbolic engagement. But on the issue of whether the Bible's historical promises are meant literally, I side with the liberal tradition.

All this is to the point of trying to understand the peace brought by the incarnation of God in Christ. That peace cannot be a historical peace. As Herod slaughtered the innocents at Jesus' birth, we continue to do that today, and with much the same dubious motive of bringing stability to the Middle East. Disparities of wealth that drive people to war and terrorism are as great today as in Jesus's time. Demonic fanaticism that attaches religious sanctions to political causes is as great today as ever. The only apocalyptic endings we can imagine are universal nuclear holocaust, destruction of the Earth's ecology, or a cosmic collision. All this is bad news if your bet is on God turning history into a comedy.

The peace that passes understanding, however, is deeper than history. The Glory of the Lord is that God is the creator of the entire cosmos, from the Big Bang to the Final Dissipation. God is the creator of our life on earth, perhaps not a grand narrative but rather countless episodes of social interactions, some connected with one another, others occurring in isolation from many other events. Within the situations pertinent to our lives we have friends and foes, and struggle to defeat the opposition to peace, justice, equity, and love. We have triumphs and failures, joys and griefs, exhilarations and suffering, births and deaths. Our lives are fragmented and often morally ambiguous. Yet we know that because God comes to us as our very Creator, we are together as God's creatures in more fundamental ways than our fragmented, ambiguous, and competitive lives might suggest. For, we are all parts of the infinitely rich divine life, eternally bound to one another in God. Although it sounds paradoxical, I am who I am in part because of the ways in which you are my other, and vice versa. You are part of my definition. Take away all the things in terms of which I define myself, and I am nothing. For each of us to be what we are, God has provided the whole cosmos.

So Jesus said you should love your neighbor as yourself. The reason is that you and your neighbor define one another, and you cannot really love yourself without loving your neighbor. Jesus said you should love your enemy. The reason is that you and your enemy define one another: to kill your enemy is to grieve his mother as yours would be grieved at your death. Jesus did not say that all things are righteous: he said that we should be in opposition to oppression, poverty, and errors of thinking that lead to suffering. But we should know that victory over others is also defeat within the larger economy that embraces both sides.

Jesus said we should love God with all our heart, mind, soul, and strength. God is not exactly like another person to whom we are connected within a common creation. God is the Creator commonly connecting us with all else. Love of God is the flip side of gratitude for our existence. But whereas gratitude can be selfish, true love of God has to acknowledge God to be the Creator of all those other things that define us, not only those others who love us but also those that hate us, not only the abundance that gives us joy but the poverty that diminishes us, not only the health that makes life a blast but the sickness that saps body and mind, not only the birth of family and friends but the death that will claim each one. God is the common source of all these things that define our glorious, fragmented, and ambiguous lives. To love this God is not easy, which is why Jesus demanded the commitment of our whole heart, mind, soul, and strength.

Nevertheless, loving God is possible precisely because God is the common Creator of us all. The light that came into the world in Jesus Christ, that little child, that refugee, that confrontational teacher, that humble man, that lover, shows us that our own depths are the depths of God. Deeper than our struggles to love neighbor is the depth and loveliness of God our common Creator. To see into these depths is the peace that passes understanding. Glory to God in the highest, and on earth peace, goodwill toward all. Amen.

14

Testimony to the Light[1]

Isaiah 60:1–6; Ephesians 3:1–12; Matthew 2:1–12

The horrendous tragedy and suffering in South and Southeast Asia this week remind us of the true context in which religion is significant. We live in a world whose natural forces, such as the tsunami, press ahead on a scale to which human affairs are trivial. Religion helps us understand humanity's place in a world of such cosmic forces. Those forces also remind us that our God, their Creator, moves on a scale that dwarfs even their terrible powers of destruction and creation. As we weep for those lives drowned out, those people depleted by sickness and grief, those futures destroyed, we need to ask, who is God whose creation breaks shorelines and their peoples like a boot on an anthill? Can human beings be at home in a creation like this?

Today is the feast of the Epiphany in the liturgical calendar, which celebrates Jesus's "appearance" to the public world. *Epiphany* means "appearance in public." The traditional gospel text for Epiphany is the familiar story of the three Wise Men who come from the East to see Jesus as one they expect to be a king. The interesting question, of course, is just what it is that appears in Jesus. Christians have always answered that it is God that is revealed in Jesus. So what does Jesus reveal of God?

Today as we struggle to reconcile the tsunami's devastation with the appearance of Baby Jesus to the delightful gift-bearing magi, I want to call

1. Preached January 2, 2005, Epiphany Sunday.

to your attention three classic Christian symbols that themselves give content to the Epiphany: that God in Jesus is the Light of the world, that God in Jesus brings salvation to all people, and that God in Jesus is King of the Universe. These are large themes, but they are all necessary to grasp the religious significance of the Epiphany.

Our text from Isaiah says, "Arise, shine; for your light has come, and the glory of the Lord has risen upon you." Last week I talked about the text from the beginning of the Gospel of John that says, "The true light, which enlightens everyone, was coming into the world." In both Isaiah and John, light symbolizes understanding. But it isn't just any old understanding. It is the understanding of the glory of God. For Isaiah, this meant something like a glory of Israel's God that would be apparent to all the nations of the Earth, so that they would come in awe and response to worship God and receive divine judgment. The theological significance of this point in Isaiah is twofold, that the God of Israel is not merely for Israel but for all nations, and that God's glory is something vaster and deeper than politics.

Christians took this passage to refer to Jesus as the light of the world. Now Jesus gave a new meaning to the divine light. On the one hand, according to John and others, the light of the world was the foundation of the creation of the world itself. The light reveals the Creator in the depth dimension of the world. On the other hand, the human meaning of Jesus as the light of the world is humility and faithfulness in love. Jesus was the one who showed God to be with the humble and poor, with those who would take last place and let others go first, with the losers in competition rather than with the hard-drivers. The light of the world never shone more starkly than at the crucifixion when the life of Jesus was snuffed out.

So as we cry for the dead and dying, the starving and grieving, we know that somehow in that suffering is the light of the world. In that suffering is the Creator, who is at once too glorious to be scaled to the concerns of human loss and too intimate not to be present in the stench and funeral pyres. Part of the Epiphany of Jesus is that we are graced by a cosmos beyond our imagining, and yet we are not alone.

Our text from Ephesians is a bit less metaphysical than the light of the world symbolism. Paul, or the author of Ephesians who was probably a student of Paul's, understood the significance of Jesus to be that by his own sacrifice, both Jews and Gentiles, all the peoples of the world, now have access to God. Moreover, they have a new common way of life, based on love, with model communities of support and worship. Paul said that Christian

Jews did not have to give up Jewish practice, and Christian Gentiles did not have to take on Jewish practice or give up their other religious life except in cases where it was synonymous with debauchery. Rather, the early Christians thought of the Christian Way as the promulgation of the good news, the gospel, that God saves all people, and that because of Jesus Christ all have access to God.

So the second thing revealed in the Epiphany of Jesus Christ is that we are all acceptable and need to find out how to live in the light of that acceptability. For Paul, and clearly for Jesus, the way to live before God is in communities of love and compassion. Surely this does not mean that only Christians should get together. It means that we who are only distantly affected by the water's devastation should take the survivors as our brothers and sisters, equally loved by God; grieve with them for the losses of their families, friends, and homes; and help them to start anew. The Epiphany lesson is that Jesus died for them as well as for us, regardless of their religious beliefs and practices.

The third symbol of God in Epiphany is that Jesus was born a king. From our text, we know that King Herod feared that what would appear in Jesus is a king who would threaten his own throne. Some of you remember from last week's gospel that Herod's reaction was to kill all the children in and around Bethlehem two years old and under, a desperate expression of his fear of alternative royalty.

We know from what followed that Jesus was not a political pretender and never became a king in Herod's sense. But Christians have claimed that Jesus was indeed a king in a more profound sense, a messiah in a sense not imagined by previous Jewish usage. The traditional word for this monarchy is Pantocrator, which means the Almighty Creator and Ruler of All. Images of Christ Pantocrator are common in Eastern Orthodox iconography, and the window above the altar here at Marsh Chapel is a somewhat domesticated version of this. The images are supposed to show how Jesus is at once human, and also the divine Logos. Christ Pantocrator is both the Alpha and the Omega. However we understand the beginning of the cosmos, its Big Bang, and its ending, perhaps a recontraction to a new Big Bang or simply a Final Dissipation of energy and order, Christ is the almighty king of that, the Cosmic King. Moreover, because God as Creator is intimately present in each thing within the flow of the cosmos, Christ Pantocrator is almighty king of that too. The Pantocrator is king of the most distant and the most intimate. Christ the King is in the death-dealing friction of tectonic plates, and also in the lost joys, the suffering, the grieving, the sickness, the hopelessness, the help, the sharing, the care, and the love in the aftermath of human disaster.

Nature's carelessness about human life causes us to ask what place we human beings have in the cosmos. The founding myths of Genesis suggest that the whole cosmos was made for the support of human life, and we know that this is not so. The cosmos is far older and vaster than anything imagined in biblical times, and we human beings have infinitesimal significance, products of mere chance evolution on a minor planet of a minor sun in a minor galaxy at the center of nothing. In the history of the Earth, last week's slight slippage of the Indian tectonic plate under the plate of Southeast Asia is a tiny part of the movement that one day will put Bombay miles beneath Bangkok. How can human beings be at home in such a cosmos?

The Epiphany of Jesus reveals that the Almighty King who creates the cosmos of unimaginable span and power is the same humble God who enjoins us to seek justice, practice mercy, to help, and to love one another. For within the vast indifference of the cosmos exists the human sphere in which justice matters, mercy matters, helping others is our calling, and love is divine. Human life is full of meaning. From the intimate tasks of working and living with family and friends to the grand tasks of social justice, world peace, the cultivation of the arts, and the attainment of high civilization, life is meaningful. Its flourishing is a joy and its destruction means tragedy. Suppose our lives are short; they still are meaningful. Suppose our communities and civilizations last only a few centuries; they still are meaningful achievements. Suppose all carbon-based life forms are extinct in a few billion years; they still will have had their eons of glory. Humanly meaningful value does not lie in lasting forever. It lies in the density with which human meaning is rooted in the depths of God.

We are at home in the universe precisely because we can care for one another and share in the meanings of one another's joys and sorrows. The vast indifference of the rest of the cosmos makes the studied care of human beings and the precious meanings of our lives all the more important. The Epiphany of Jesus Christ, Pantocrator, King of the Universe, reveals this.

I invite you, then, to squint with me in the light that reveals God's glory so vast and cosmic that the psalmist asks in amazement, "What is man that Thou art mindful of him?" We cannot deny the brightness of that glory by seeking to make God a domestic caretaker of the human scale of things. That same light, however, is the humble Jesus who illuminates the folds of justice, mercy, and love. I invite you also to accept Ephesians' call to recognize that all people lie within the creative love of God and are free to approach God's glory as redeemed sinners. Let us have no partisanship about who our brothers and sisters are, and where we all are going. I invite you finally to join the Wise Men in adoration of the Baby Jesus, helpless in the bosom of his family, nearly killed by imperial dynastic politics, finally killed by a later stage of that same imperial process. For, what that baby will teach is how to be at home as lovers of God and one another in a cosmos for which human life is wondrously strange and worthy. Come to the table where the light illumines God's glory and our ties with all the people of God's creation. Amen

15

The Name of Jesus[1]: Baptism of the Lord

Isaiah 42:1–9; Acts 10:31–43; Matthew 3:11–17

The beautiful passage from Isaiah 42 that was our Hebrew Bible text this morning is the first of four "Servant Songs," as the scholars call them. These are songs or poems in which the nation of Israel is personified as a servant, "upheld," "chosen," and "delighted in" by God. The work of Israel as servant is to go for God to all the nations of the world and bring them to justice. This will not be done by force but quietly and subtly: "He will not cry or lift up his voice, or make it heard in the street; a bruised reed he will not break, and a dimly burning wick he will not quench; he will faithfully bring forth justice." The servant role of Israel is to "bring forth justice" among all the nations of the world. God says to servant Israel, "I am the Lord, I have called you in righteousness, I have taken you by the hand and kept you; I have given you as a covenant to the people, a light to the nations, to open the eyes that are blind, to bring out the prisoners from the dungeon, from prison those who sit in darkness." Israel should not live only for itself before God, as was the theme of the Sinai covenant with Moses. Now God says that Israel itself is given to the other nations as a covenant to bring all the world's people to justice. Israel is to be God's righteous servant sent to the world.

---

1. Preached January 9, 2005, the Sunday celebrating the Baptism of the Lord.

The early Christians seized upon this and the other Servant Songs to refer, not to the whole people of Israel as personified, but to the messiah, namely, Jesus. Perhaps other Jewish groups identified the servant with an individual messiah, not with the nation. But the portrait in the Servant Songs seemed to fit what happened to Jesus rather than any successful kingly messiah of the sort that the others hoped for. The fourth Servant Song, at Isaiah 53, says things such as "he had no form or majesty that we should look at him, nothing in his appearance that we should desire him. He was despised and rejected by others; a man of suffering and acquainted with infirmity.... Surely he has borne our infirmities and carried our diseases; yet we accounted him stricken, struck down by God, and afflicted. But he was wounded for our transgressions, crushed for our iniquities; upon him was the punishment that made us whole, and by his bruises we are healed." That description might well apply to poor battered Israel, as Isaiah saw the scene. But it also could be applied to Jesus, the crucified teacher of justice and peace whom the early Christians believed had redeemed them in his very humility and suffering. Jesus did not fit the description of a mighty military messiah like David at all. The early Christians looked to the Servant Songs to redefine what it means to be the messiah. It means to suffer as Jesus did to bring the rest of the world to justice, bearing "the sins of many."

Think now of the gospel lesson, Jesus's baptism. John the Baptist had been preaching repentance of injustice and the imminence of God's kingdom that would establish justice. Jesus came to John for baptism, recognizing John's prophetic authority and committing himself in faith to the justice John preached. When Jesus came up out of the water, he had that astonishing vision: "suddenly the heavens were opened to him and he saw the Spirit of God descending like a dove and alighting on him. And a voice from heaven said, 'This is my Son, the Beloved, with whom I am well pleased.'" That was a life-transforming religious experience, if I might use that almost trivial phrase for what Jesus went through. Doubtless he remembered the Isaiah passage, "Here is my servant, whom I uphold, my chosen, in whom my soul delights," and he then understood his mission: to bring forth justice among the nations. Perhaps it took Jesus a while to recognize the full extent of that mission. Originally he had thought it was to Israel only. But Matthew ends his gospel with Jesus commissioning the disciples to go to all nations, not Israel alone.

Paul understood the significance of Jesus to be for the salvation of the Gentiles as well as the Jews. Peter said, according to our Epistle lesson, "I

The Name of Jesus: Baptism of the Lord

truly understand that God shows no partiality, but in every nation anyone who fears him and does what is right is acceptable to him. You know the message he sent to the people of Israel, preaching peace by Jesus Christ—he is Lord of all . . . All the prophets testify about him that everyone who believes in him receives forgiveness of sins through his name." Peter said this in a sermon addressed to Gentiles.

Now we Christians take on the name of Jesus in our own baptism. Becoming Christians, we are "of Christ." What does this mean? Two answers are very important to this question.

The first, and less important, is that by taking on the name of Jesus Christ we enter into the cult of Jesus, the church. By "cult" I don't mean a small extremist religious group, but rather a religious community that cultivates a special way of life. We ourselves are cultivated to be better Christians through participating in our community, the church. Included in that cultivation is belief in certain things about Jesus, and celebrating the significance of his life through the festivals of the liturgical year—today is the feast of the Baptism of Jesus. Christian cultivation is of the way of life he taught, emphasizing justice, peace, forgiveness, and love.

The second, and more important, answer to the question of what it means for us to bear the name of Jesus Christ is that we are God's servants to the world to bring forth justice, as Isaiah said. Justice for us is a large notion, enriched by Jesus's entire teaching to contain peace, mercy, forgiveness, humility, care for the poor, relief of suffering, love in all ways appropriate to people in different situations. To "believe in" Jesus does not mean only to join in the cult of Jesus. It means also and more importantly to believe in and join his servant mission. Isaiah's servant did not live for himself but served God by extending himself to suffer for the world. Jesus did the same thing. To believe in Jesus is to live for God's work of justice, peace, mercy, forgiveness, humility, care for the poor, relief of suffering, and love in and for all nations.

One of the main problems we Christians have is that it is so easy to live for the church, aiming to make it flourish, rather than for the world. The purpose of the church is to cultivate us just enough that we take on the life and work of Jesus whose name we bear. We need to hear and understand the word of God regarding justice; we need to cultivate the virtues of redeemed and sanctified people; we need to practice love of one another and develop supportive communities. Those of us in the religion business, such as I, spend a lot of time trying to get the church in such shape as to be able to cultivate these powers for the mission of justice. Yet we should know, as often we do not, that the church does not live for itself, but for its mission, which is to the world. We should never forget the world when we devote our energies to building up the church. The church needs always to empty itself for the sake of the world.

Some Christians, from the very earliest times, have thought that believing in Jesus Christ means mainly joining up as Christians. They have emphasized conversion and belonging more than the mission to those who suffer injustice and might not belong to Christ. They are more concerned about getting people to become Christians than doing the Christian work of bringing justice to the world. I believe this is a mistaken and dangerous emphasis within Christianity.

Other Christians, including myself, have construed membership in the church as mainly instrumental to fostering the real mission of Jesus, the suffering servant. Because so many people in other religions also pursue justice, a Christian's true solidarity sometimes is more with them, because that is Christ's mission however they understand it, than it is with those whose mission is mainly to get people to become Christians. Truly to believe in Jesus Christ is to be committed to his mission, and all those who are committed to justice are true believers, even if they do not use Christian language or know about Jesus Christ. They do not have to become Christians to take on Jesus's identity as the servant of God for justice across the world.

So I am sadly suspicious of Christians who talk of conversion before emptying themselves in the pursuit of justice. It is absurd for Christians to want to convert Jews, because Jews already have Isaiah and his mission that Jesus seized for his own identity. Christian can encourage Jews to become better Jews. And is it not scandalous that some Christians now look upon the devastation in Afghanistan and Iraq first as opportunities to convert Muslims to Christianity and only secondarily, if at all, as crying needs to bring forth justice, "to open the eyes that are blind, to bring out the prisoners from the dungeon, from the prison those who sit in darkness"?

America has brought forth vast and cruel injustice in the Middle East, attacking two nations that did not attack us, for no reasons that stand examination, destroying not only their governments but also the infrastructures of their societies, leading to the ready threat of civil war. We treat the people who object to this unjust imperialism, and fight back, as our enemies rather than as colleagues seeking justice. We give new meaning to prisoners in dungeons and their torture, and seek to promote the people who justify such torture to higher office. And much of this evil, that Jesus would have called Satanic, is supported by Christians who seem to care more about converting others to Christianity than Christ's mission of justice! How can the name of Jesus Christ be so perverted?!

Of course these political and ethical matters are very complex. Tribal and religious conflicts within both Afghanistan and Iraq complicate the insurgency against American occupation. Moreover, many American people support American imperial aggression inadvertently when they only want to attack gay marriage, stem cell research, or women's rights to determine whether they will carry a child. Despite these complications and ambiguities, the Christian influence on American policy and public life should always be first and foremost to bring forth justice among all the nations, where justice means the rich panoply of conditions about which Jesus preached.

Just as the early Christians adopted and adapted Isaiah's personification of the people of Israel as a suffering servant to understand the significance of Jesus Christ, so we need to look back to Isaiah's priorities for that servant to correct our understanding of the work of those who bear the name of Jesus Christ. Of course we need to foster the church, the cult of Jesus Christ, in order to take on his mind, to cultivate the virtues necessary for the pursuit of justice, peace, humility, mercy, forgiveness, care for the poor, relief for the suffering, and love in all its forms. We need the church for the support necessary to witness against the injustice of our own government and to provide a countervailing force for justice in other parts of the world. But we do not need the church when it fails Christ's mission of justice. As Jesus said in the Gospel of John, the branches of the true vine that do not bear fruit should be pruned away. Christianity that exists for its own sake is a sucker on the vine that saps the energy of the messiah and those who bear his name. We need scrupulous vigilance to root out those seductive images of salvation that make it seem a matter primarily of being on the right side, merely of joining up, only of belonging to the cult, mainly of converting from a different religious identity. Our Christian life does not truly begin until we find ourselves part of the body that carries on Christ's mission of justice for the nations. What is the concrete meaning of salvation? It is to do justice, have mercy, and walk humbly with our God.

When Jesus rose from baptism, he saw the heavens open, saw God's spirit descend like a dove, and heard God claim him as a beloved son. May we who bear the name of Jesus Christ understand that our identity as servants of justice has its roots in God, not politics, and share Jesus's confirming vision. Amen.

16

Light, Vocation, Healing[1]

Isaiah 9:1–3; 1 Corinthians 1:11–18; Matthew 4:11–23

Matthew's Gospel quotes our text from Isaiah: "the people who sat in darkness have seen a great light, and for those who sat in the region and shadow of death, light has dawned." The image of light is one of the great figures of Western religion, as well as Buddhism and Hinduism, the religions of South Asia, and it has many meanings. Like most of the important symbols of religion, its many meanings resonate with one another and reinforce its power far beyond the significance of any one of its meanings.

In Isaiah, the principal meaning of the light that has dawned is that the people who sat in the darkness of political oppression have now been visited by the glory of God and they shall prosper as at the hand of the messiah. Light is a symbol of divine glory and favor. Matthew spins this passage to mean that the special favor God bestows on Zebulun and Naphtali, the territory of Capernaum where Jesus established his permanent home, is that the messiah saving the whole world has come from there. The glory of Zebulun and Naphtali is not necessarily that they will become especially just and prosperous as Isaiah said, but that they have the honor of being the home of Jesus the Messiah. As history would have it, Jesus would be known as the Nazarene, where he grew through the teen and young adult years, not as Jesus of Capernaum, nor as Jesus of Bethlehem, his birthplace, or Jesus

---

1. Preached January 23rd, 2005, the third Sunday after Epiphany.

of Egypt where he spent his early years. Nevertheless, the light shone with divine favor on Capernaum, of Zebulun and Naphtali.

The symbol of divine light also means the source of the good example and teaching. Other passages in Isaiah that we have discussed in previous weeks said that Israel as the Suffering Servant would be the light to the nations, showing them the glory of God and instructing them in justice. Jesus has this meaning of light in mind when, in the fifth chapter of Matthew, in the Sermon on the Mount, he says to the crowd, "You are the light of the world. A city built on a hill cannot be hid. No one after lighting a lamp puts it under the bushel basket, but on the lampstand, and it gives light to all in the house. In the same way, let your light shine before others, so that they may see your good works and give glory to your Father in heaven." I have great affection for this biblical meaning of light because, when I was very small my mother taught me my first song—"A sunbeam, a sunbeam, Jesus wants me for a sunbeam." As I got older and matured in the arts of sin, she amended her teaching, saying "Don't show off so much, Bobby!" What's cute at three is pretentious in a ten-year-old who proclaims himself a sunbeam for Jesus. My experience illustrates the difficulty in being the light of the world. When the Puritans came to America to establish the city built on a hill to be a light to the rest of the world, they soon were dazzled by their own self-righteousness. We in America, deeply committed to being the glory of God, are still working through that self-righteous bedazzlement.

Yet another biblical meaning of light, perhaps the most profound yet, is divine understanding. As we have quoted several times in the last month, the beginning of John's Gospel says that Jesus was the light of all people. Then recalling our Isaiah text, John says, "The light shines in the darkness, and the darkness did not overcome it." The light, according to John, is the Word of God through which all creation has come to be. That Word, *Logos* in Greek, is the divine mind, the understanding or intelligibility at the heart of God through which the cosmos and its goodness can be understood. One of the primary ways that we can love God is through understanding God through the Word. This spiritual path is especially beloved of theologians, and I acknowledge a professional bias here. Nevertheless, the spiritual path of understanding and meditation, of striving for a vision of God, is at the center of the Christian, and most other religious traditions.

The Christians discovered very early that approaching the divine light for understanding can be easily misconstrued. Many early Christians, and Jews too, thought that by focusing on the knowledge of God they could leave earthly concerns and climb to a higher reality. Perhaps you've known mystics who are bit too otherworldly. These people were condemned under the name of being gnostics. Gnosticism is the officially heretical belief that one can be saved from the world by special knowledge of higher planes of reality. The orthodox Christian point, made directly by John, is just the opposite: the Word came into the world and we find its saving light here. Salvation is not escape from the world, but the discovery of God in the world.

Why should we study science? Not principally for better technology, but to understand the world God has created and worship the Creator that way. Why should we cultivate and study the arts? Not principally for decoration, but to explore God's beauty in the world and give it residence in our lives. Why should we ponder the meaning of life? Because that is God calling us to find the divine meaning and intelligence within our very selves.

John, like Matthew and Isaiah, contrasts the light with the darkness, which has not overcome it. For our Isaiah text, darkness meant the horrors of suffering under the vicious rule of the Assyrians who occupied Zebulun and Naphtali, and light meant messianic relief. For Matthew, the darkness probably symbolizes human sin, for he has Jesus preach, "Repent, for the kingdom of heaven has come near." Those are the exact same words Matthew put in John the Baptist's mouth in the previous chapter. The darkness of human sin is about to be shone up by the light of the Messiah, and so repent quickly. For John, the darkness symbolizes all evil, cosmic as well as human. That evil cannot overcome the light of God that has come into the very place of evil itself.

This leads to the last meaning of the biblical symbol of divine light, namely, that it reveals who and what we are, our shame as well as glory, our dirty secrets as well as our virtue. Paul, in the fourth chapter of 1 Corinthians, warning people not to judge one another, says, "Therefore do not pronounce judgment before the time, before the Lord comes, who will bring to light the things now hidden in darkness and will disclose the purposes of the heart." In our own souls, the light that reveals all is at war with the darkness that would keep things hidden. Light exposes us. It shows the God within us. And it shows the darkness that is a rejection of light. Light is God coming to us, but it is very scary. In so many things, we prefer the dark. The light of the world makes us honest.

The Christian moral is that to embrace Christ is to pursue the light. To pursue the light is to be grateful for our blessings, in contrast to the Assyrian alternative. To pursue the light is to rejoice that Christ's messianic mission rests with us: like Zebulun and Naphtali, we are hosts for God's work. To pursue the light is to embrace the work of being the light of the world, the sunbeam, the beacon, the help to others struggling to understand and live well. To pursue the light means to commit ourselves to knowledge, to inquiry, to creativity in accord with God's Word. To pursue the light means finally to become honest and admit who we are.

Honesty is always easier to require in others. So we can be easy with the Christian duty to shine the light of truth on government rhetoric in which democracy means capitalism, freedom means occupation, liberation means control by us, insurgents means freedom fighters, compassionate conservatism means cutting entitlements, social security means betting on the market, "no child left behind" means those who are not already behind, international cooperation means our way or not at all, and morality means the imposition of one culture on everyone. Let's be honest about "them."

It's harder to be honest about the ways we live ourselves, for whom pension funds require management to squeeze out top dollar; ourselves, for whom freedom to spend what we acquire requires occupying countries who object; ourselves, for whom gasoline consumption requires control of the oil; ourselves, for whom defense of our children in the military requires demonizing those who attempt to expel them from their countries; ourselves, who do not want to pay taxes for entitlements to help the poor; ourselves, for whom a satisfactory way of life requires a system in which others are left behind in satisfaction; ourselves, for whom giving up American sovereignty might cost us our way of life; ourselves, who prefer our culture's morals to others and act to impose them. Let's be honest about ourselves and how our government so often speaks for our real but dark interests if not for our better sentiments.

Let me only hint at a further honesty required in the light of Jesus, a candle in the heart of our souls. Do we secretly want a control of others that borders on sadism? Do we secretly want to embrace the lie that we are better than others, knowing it is a lie? Do we secretly lust after wealth, power, and flesh, not merely enjoy those things, but lust after them? Do we secretly want comfort and plenty rather than the duty that comes from the watch in which God stations us? Do we secretly long continually to test God's love, because we do not love ourselves properly? Do we secretly want to give ourselves to the powers that might give us our secret passions rather than to the God whose light exposes those passions? Surely I dare not speak for anyone here, including myself. The last three of those secret passions are

Light, Vocation, Healing

those to which Satan appealed in Jesus during the temptation, and I suspect the devil is a pretty good judge of our character too. Nevertheless, the light of God is here among us. God's glory is here. And we are exposed.

The good news is that we therefore have a vocation. In Matthew's text, Jesus called Peter and Andrew, James and John, and told them he would make them fishers of people. We are those who have been caught, and like those disciples we have been called to follow Jesus. Peter, Andrew, James, and John were not better than we are. They too had a dubious government that gave them peace and a good living, and their hearts were as secretly corrupt as our own. No matter, says the gospel. That doesn't matter. All is forgiven if you get up and follow. The darkness of our society is no excuse to sit still. The darkness of our dependence on darkness is no excuse to sit still. The darkness of our souls is no excuse to refuse the call. "Follow me, and I will make you fish for people." That is our vocation, freely given, and giving of freedom. That is the gospel, the good news.

So where did the disciples follow Jesus? The text says Jesus went about teaching in the "synagogues and proclaiming the good news of the kingdom and curing every disease and every sickness among the people." Our vocation is to follow along and do that too. Even in our darkness we can proclaim the light that is God's glory and that exposes the sins of which we and everyone else should repent. We teach by word and example that the darkness cannot overcome the light. And then we help people, curing every disease and sickness. That does not mean only biological sickness. It means the sickness of injustice, poverty, war, arrogance, power madness, selfishness, and hate. Of course the ways to cure these things are obscure. Of course the sicknesses remain in us. Yet the Christian good news is that these things cannot keep us down. We have the light that shows us a vision of justice. We have the light that allows us to imagine sharing wealth with everyone. We have the light to wage peace, to curb power madness, and selfishness. We have the light to turn hate to love. For the light of the world has dwelt among us in Jesus and even death could not turn that light to darkness. We who have dwelt in darkness have seen a great light. Let us enter into that light that has come to us. Amen

17

To Know What Counts[1]

Micah 6:1–8; 1 Corinthians 1:11–31; Matthew 5:1–12

To be wise is to know what counts in life. On the surface, this means knowing what to value, and what values should guide life. Deeper down, knowing what counts includes knowing the way the world works, what the deep patterns of causation are, how to tell the roots from the branches, what to expect when you pursue your values and your neighbors pursue theirs, and what the prices are for commitment to what really counts. Bach's music is wise

Our texts this morning address three dimensions of wisdom.

The first, from Micah, is the rock bottom and is presupposed by the rest. "And what does the LORD require of you but to do justice, and to love kindness, and to walk humbly with your God?" Justice, kindness, humility. The Big Three. Justice is complicated, of course, and sometimes we have difficulty figuring out the just path. Micah's point is not to simplify justice but rather to say, whatever justice is, and we do indeed know what it is in the vast majority of situations, do it. I often use the old Book of Common Prayer for morning or evening devotions, and the 1662 version begins with this sentence from Ezekiel (18:27): "When the wicked man turneth away from his wickedness that he hath committed, and doeth that which is lawful and right, he shall save his soul alive." No excuses. No temporizing.

---

1. Preached January 30, 2005, the fourth Sunday after Epiphany. Bach's Cantata no. 40 was performed.

No appeals to ambiguity or understandable weakness: just do it. That plain statement sometimes stops me with tears, until I can remember God's mercy that helps me face what I cannot face by myself. Then I rush on to the part of the service about confession and absolution.

"Love kindness," says Micah. The older translations often have "love mercy," and I think a whole host of connotations are intended here that add up to what Christians have come to call love. "Love love," is what this clause means. Do justice, but love love. To be sure, this means that we should be loving just as we should be just. In addition, however, Micah enjoins us to prize loving-kindness as the most important personal trait. One can do justice while still being hateful or indifferent. To be kind, merciful, and loving, however, is a special condition of the heart. Jesus did not invent the love ethic as something to supersede the Jewish justice ethic, as some Christians have believed. For Micah the prophet, justice should define our behavior and loving-kindness should define our hearts.

The reason the Bible advocates justice and mercy as what count fundamentally for human life is that it takes those traits to characterize God. God is just and merciful, and demands justice and mercy from us. We might be a little wary about this anthropomorphic view of God as a just and merciful king—God is so much greater than that. Nevertheless, the God who creates the world, in which standards of justice and loving-kindness measure who we are in the perspective of eternity, can easily and inevitably be symbolized as just and mercifully loving. Not to do so, in fact, would be to fail to take justice and loving-kindness seriously enough to define what counts in life.

"To walk humbly with your God," the third thing that counts, would not seem to be a divine trait to which human beings are called. Rather humility is taken to define our very relation to God. To put the point in modern terms, how are we to present ourselves in ultimate perspective? Humbly. How should we behave when ultimate matters are at hand? Not arrogantly. Not bragging about our skills or accomplishments. Not even beating our breasts and crying for forgiveness. We should simply be humble. Humility is the attitude of heart by which we should face God: otherwise we do not know what we face.

Christians go so far as to say that humility, like justice and loving-kindness, is indeed a trait of God. When we have failed at justice, love, and humility, God calls us back with the humility of Jesus who, as Paul put it in Philippians 2, "though he was in the form of God, did not regard equality with God as something to be exploited, but emptied himself, taking the form of a slave, being born in human likeness. And being found in human form, he humbled himself and became obedient to the point of death—even death on a cross." Jesus could break through to the unjust, unloving, and arrogant folks precisely because he was willing to be humble himself. Jesus showed us how to relate to God: with perfect humility. How can we keep God with us in our walk through life? By walking humbly with God.

Of course most of us are not very just, do not love kindness very far beyond the circle of our friends, and are not very humble, waffling as we do between arrogance and self-hate. Or rather, to put the point more humbly, we Christians are still only on the path to justice, love, and humility when our worst enemies are ourselves and the ways of life we have come to prize. Because we have the mind and example of Jesus Christ, and the witness of saints through the ages, there really is no excuse for us to fail at the effort of living wisely. Appearances to the contrary notwithstanding, it is not beyond our reach to do justice, love kindness, and walk humbly with our God.

Yet as Paul said in the lectionary text from 1 Corinthians that we did not read, this gospel that sets us free for justice, love, and humility is bafflingly counterintuitive. The humility of Jesus to be crucified is a stumbling block to the Jews, Paul said, who expected the Messiah to come with shock and awe, and foolishness to the Gentiles who expected a philosopher. This is the second dimension of wisdom from our texts: our ability as Christians to be just, loving, and humble requires the special humility of faith in what God has chosen as means of grace. "God chose what is low and despised in the world, things that are not, to reduce to nothing things that are, so that no one might boast in the presence of God." It is the problem of humility again. We are prone to boast instead. Yet what has God done for us? God taught us justice, love, and humility in the example of Jesus. Thank goodness, religions other than Christianity also acknowledge the wisdom of justice, loving-kindness, and humility.

The third dimension of wisdom in our texts is Jesus's own teaching of the Beatitudes. Jesus goes beyond Micah to say that the just, loving, and humble are happy. That is the basic meaning of "blessed": happy. Happiness in this sense does not necessarily mean filled with enjoyment. Jesus means rather that people with these characters are happy in their relation with God: those who are poor in spirit, those who mourn, the meek, the merciful, the seekers after justice, the pure in heart, the peacemakers, and those persecuted for righteousness' sake.

In worldly ways, the people whom Jesus calls blessed are probably not happy. Although people have debated for two thousand years just what Jesus had in mind by these traits, they all signal humility, a mournful sensitivity to the suffering of others, responsibility for others so that mercy might be called for, a thirst for righteousness we feel we do not have, the hard discipline of integrating and pruning one's desires so as to have a pure heart, a willingness to sacrifice one's interest in order to make peace, and the lonely courage to stand for righteousness in ways that draw down persecution.

During many periods of Christian history, those Jesus called blessed were regarded as wimps. Christians have not always attended to Christian virtues. The opposite of those who are poor in spirit are those with overweening confidence in their religiosity. The opposite of those who mourn for suffering are those who dismiss suffering as collateral damage in the pursuit of their interests. The opposite of the merciful are those who believe their own righteousness excludes the righteousness of their opponents. The opposite of those who thirst for righteousness are those who declare they have it. The opposite of the pure in heart are those who deceive themselves and lie to others to accomplish confused and dark ends. The opposite of the peacemakers are those who believe their righteousness justifies unprovoked war. The opposite of those persecuted for righteousness' sake are those who persecute for their righteousness' sake. We have many people in our land who proudly hold opposite traits to the Beatitudes, perhaps even a majority of those who call themselves Christians, all in the name of their own righteousness. Perhaps they are happy in worldly ways of aggressive pursuit of their cultural and economic interests while feeling good about themselves.

But they are not happy in the ways of presenting themselves to God as just, loving, and humble. In the ultimate perspective of the great Creator of this vast, unmeasured universe, whose main movements are blasts of stellar gasses, and whose islands of hospitality for life are surrounded by cold vacuum, the pomp of human arrogance and self-righteousness is a cosmic pratfall, a joke, an abomination. In ultimate perspective the only way to be happy is to walk humbly with the Creator, to do justice wherever we can, and to prize the loving-kindness that binds us together against the dark and links us to God before whom all other walks of life are foolish offense.

As we listen to Bach, I invite you to feel the lines of his music that seem to come to us from nature far beyond the human spheres and to extend forever beyond our performance, linking us in cosmic loving-kindness. I invite you to hear in his music the complexity that models the intertwining of life in which justice consists. I invite you to understand in his music the signal that the greatest of human achievements is to be humble before the face of God. This is what counts. Amen.

18

Coping with Transfiguration[1]

Exodus 24:11–18; 2 Peter 1:11–21; Matthew 17:1–9

The Feast of the Transfiguration, which is the formal name for this Sunday in the liturgical calendar, celebrates one of the more weird events in Christian history. After Peter had declared that Jesus was the Messiah—six days after according to Matthew and Mark, eight days for Luke—Jesus took Peter, James, and John up a mountain and was transfigured before their eyes, his body and clothing becoming radiant. Moreover, the disciples saw him talking with Moses and Elijah. Peter offered to make temporary shelters for Jesus, Moses, and Elijah, an offer not taken up. Then a bright cloud came over the mountain and a voice spoke from the cloud saying, "This is my Son, the Beloved; with him I am well pleased; listen to him." The disciples fell to the ground, and Jesus came over and touched them with instructions not to be afraid. When they looked, Moses and Elijah were gone.

What does this mean, besides a physical transformation that computer graphics could easily duplicate today, right down to the appearance of Moses and Elijah? Part of the meaning lies in the reference to Moses. Our text from Exodus recounts Moses going up Mount Sinai to receive the covenant; on the peak God's presence is like a bright cloud that cannot be approached but through which God blesses the people. When Moses went back down the mountain, his face was transfigured to shine so brightly that it frightened the people. For Christians, Moses brought the first covenant

---

1. Preached February 2, 2005; Transfiguration Sunday.

and Jesus the second or new covenant. Matthew's transfiguration passage affirms the continuity of the covenants from Moses to Jesus, thus running contrary to those who believe that Jesus's covenant was a rejection of Moses's covenant rather than a continuous supplement.

Another part of the meaning of the transfiguration comes out in Peter's eyewitness recollection of the event, in the Epistle this morning. Peter referred to the transfiguration as a counter to the charge that Jesus was something like a pagan god, filled with magic. However magical the transfiguration was, Peter said he was there and saw it. Moreover, he saw Moses and Elijah, both long dead. This demonstrated to him the resurrection of the dead. Not only was Jesus raised, he would come again, just as Moses and Elijah came again. The transfiguration was thus a foretaste of resurrected life.

Yet another part of the meaning of Jesus's transfiguration is that the disciples saw Jesus as approved by God. The voice, which the people took to be God's, identified Jesus as God's son in whom God was well pleased. These were the same words heard when Jesus was baptized by John. At the baptism, Jesus was transformed. At the transfiguration, the disciples were transformed.

What does all this mean for us today? I doubt many of us take this as a literal happening that somehow proves Jesus's divinity, although that is how the story was taken for centuries. To our skeptical minds it seems too much like a dream, and Luke actually says that the disciples were falling asleep when the vision came.

Let me ask you, however, whether you have ever had experiences in which your world suddenly was transfigured and shown to be vastly more profound, astonishing, and divine than you had thought. When I was thirteen, my high school English teacher was talking with me about religion after class and remarked, "You know, Bob, that God is not in time." I was astonished by that remark, astonished to have encountered a totally new and unusual thought, astonished that I understood it, and astonished to see suddenly into the intellectual world in which I knew then I would live the rest of my life. When I was a college student, I worked in a Boy Scout camp as chaplain in the summers. One night, as I lay on the deserted parade ground looking up at the star-filled night sky, suddenly I saw through that vision to an infinity of creation incomprehensibly old and vast in which I had my own particular place, a divine meeting ground of the infinite and the finite, or more prosaically, of God and me. Later in college I came to the sudden realization that the pastor of my church when I was in high school had been a saint, not just the kindly man who brought me into ministry, but a saint; what a transfiguration of my adolescence that realization was, to have been in the presence of a saint! In graduate school I was working on the philosophical problem of divine creation and one day, confused and in emotional and intellectual agony, I knelt by my rickety chair to pray —dirty yellow in the pseudo-Danish Modern style. Suddenly all my thinking fell together and I grasped my complex theory of divine creation like a vast name of God, and that name let my prayer engage God as I had never before: I perceived God as creator. And so came more little transfigurations. About a dozen years ago I was visualizing Jesus as a revelation of God and pictured him running up a hill, nearing the verge, with a crowd including myself running behind him, knowing that when we topped the verge we would see God. Again and again we ran up, never reaching the top. At last we followed Jesus over the brow of the hill and I fell into a comprehension of how God contains the present, past, and future all together, not in time but in the creation of time, a divine life infinitely more dynamic than our passing of days within time. The intellectual theory, of course, was my own construction, but the transfiguring experience was to think and feel God through it. To this day it takes me about three hours to think or meditate myself into grasping that complex idea plus the visualization of Jesus that allows me to engage God by that means, and I very rarely have that much concentrated time. But every time, it is a transfiguration of my experience.

I wager that many of you have had transfiguring experiences in which something ordinary and everyday suddenly becomes luminous to reveal something extraordinary and life-transforming. Astonishing sunsets, the primeval heave of the ocean, transcendent music, the birth of a baby, someone's touch at the right time, the bottoming out of despair, a sudden strange empathy with people to whom you are not connected: most of you have had personal experiences that set you outside the ordinary and give you a temporary new grasp on reality. Not all transfiguring experiences are happy and uplifting, to be sure. The world in which my wife and I lived was radically transfigured when our daughter died in infancy, and we have spent nearly forty years coming to terms with that. Some people's worlds are transfigured by madness, which is disconnected from the rest of reality. Theologians such as Paul Tillich call these "ecstatic" experiences, moments of ecstasy that figuratively make us stand outside ourselves in a new reality;

"ecstasy" literally means standing outside oneself. Experiences such as these are little transfigurations.

How do we cope with these little transfigurations? They usually do not last long and they get submerged in ordinary reality when we come back down the mountain. When Jesus went back down in the morning, he had to plunge right in to deal with a botched healing that his other, less than competent, disciples had attempted in his absence. Often we do not understand our transfigurations at the time, as the disciples did not understand Jesus's transfiguration until after his death and resurrection. Sometimes these experiences are so delicious that we classify them as aesthetic and lift them out of life into irrelevance. Or they are so terrifying and horrible that they are dangerous to our sense of secure ordinary reality, and we try to deny, repress, and forget them. Few of us have grand life-shattering mystical experiences. Mostly we get along rather with small passing ecstasies to which we might give little or no importance.

Friends, let me suggest that we cope with our transfigurations as windows through which to see God and what is ultimately important. Those transfigurations become like ideas or signs by which we can discern realities that are opaque to us without those signs. Like an NMR machine that creates a television picture of your insides out of perturbations in a magnetic field, these transfiguration experiences are signs that make it possible for us to engage what ordinary experience hides. These transfigurations give us the language, the images, the tools, with which we can recognize and relate to extraordinary dimensions of reality. By their means we can interpret aspects of reality that otherwise we would miss.

The transfigurations of life are engagements with the depth dimensions of reality. But they themselves need to be understood as interpretations engaging reality. If we look at the experiences themselves, taken out of their interpretive roles in engaging ultimate matters, they can be silly or just madness. Perhaps they are only dreams, fictions, intellectual constructs in my case. Ecstatic experiences can be caused by epilepsy or LSD or whirling in a circle, and they mean nothing in themselves. Nevertheless, if we cope with them, not in themselves, but as parts of existential acts of engaging things deeper than the ordinary, they can become the symbols that throw us together with those deep matters. The literal meaning of "symbol" is "to throw together," to engage. Like all matters of the Spirit, the problem is to discern the spirits to see whether these transfigurations are of the Holy Spirit. The long-run test is whether they lead to the life of love, peace, and graciousness. The short-run tests have to do with whether they give meaning to our lives as genuine engagements with reality's ordinarily hidden depths. Part of the work of the Holy Spirit in our lives, or of our task of holiness, is to find ways to live with the blazing colors of the extraordinary reality of our wild God at the same time that we live with the muted colors of ordinary life, within which we lie under obligation, and without which life would be chaos.

I invite you, therefore, to treasure your transfigurations, meditate on them, ask what you might learn from them. Let them be a lesson that our ordinary thoughts paint reality with dull colors so that we can deal with the practical dimensions of life. The transfiguring experiences teach us that God's blinding colors truly can be seen and loved, if only for a moment, and only with weird images that ordinary life cannot stand to take seriously.

Many of us have seen this pita bread and port wine transfigured into the body and blood of Jesus. Truly, this is sometimes a vision, not just a doctrine. Perhaps we have also peered beyond to the next window and seen the body and blood of Jesus transfigured to be God's merciful purification, God's food, God's love, God's depth, God's glory. I invite you to trust your transfigurations and, like the disciples, to wait upon the understanding of them. Come to this mountaintop meal. In the name of the Father, the Son, and the Holy Spirit. Amen.

19

Ash Wednesday[1]

Joel 2:12, 11–17; 2 Corinthians 5:20b—6:10;
Matthew 6: 1–6, 11–21

The people who assembled the Revised Common Lectionary from which the Ash Wednesday readings are drawn obviously had some unfinished business. On the very day in which we mark our foreheads with the sign of the cross to indicate our acknowledgment of sins, and penance, they give us the passage from Matthew where Jesus condemns doing such things. Jesus says overt marks of penitence are hypocritical and that we should appear to others as if it were any other day. God who sees in secret is enough. This passage stands in stark contrast to Paul's remarks in the Epistle to the Corinthians about the pains of being steady witnesses to Christ. Perhaps the lectionary mavens wanted us to choose between the two attitudes. Perhaps the committee was dominated by free-church Christians who abominate high-church rituals such as the imposition of ashes as idolatrizing Romanism. At any rate, we need to finish the business and think through this day of overt expression of faith, contrition, and resolution.

The key, I believe, is in the reading from Joel. The day of the Lord is coming, says Joel, a day of devastating judgment. Joel construes a devastating plague of locusts, which was destroying the economy of Israel, to be a divine judgment against Israel for her sins. He likens the locusts to the

1. Preached February 9, 2005, Ash Wednesday.

Ash Wednesday

armies of Assyrians and Babylonians that in previous centuries had devastated the land and carried off many of the inhabitants. The prophets also construed those disasters as punishments for Israel's sins.

Now I do not believe that God starves out people, including innocent children, and ruins environments to punish idolaters who worship gods other than Yahweh, which was the issue in Joel's imagination. The locusts came because they woke from their seventeen-year hibernation. Nor are the military adventures of the Egyptians, Assyrians, Babylonians, and Persians to be interpreted as punishments for Israel. The prophets were put in a bind by their own theology, which was that the God of Israel guaranteed protection and special status for Israel. If Israel suffered from political or natural disasters, this could not be because God was weak or unfaithful. The prophets had to lay moral blame on Israel. That is the bad theology that comes from thinking of the Creator as a small, partisan deity. We know God to be the infinite creator of billions of galaxies, a God whose creation is wild from the perspective of human ambitions, a God whose love is more fecund, and intimate to our souls, than the vengeful, political God of Joel's imagination.

Nevertheless, Joel was right that actions have consequences for our relations with God. When we hurt other people, we deny the plain truth that they are equally children of God. When we neglect prayer and worship, we become distant from the intimate ground of our being. When we move through life half asleep, we deny that everything created glistens with the pulse of God's creation. When we are inattentive to the life around us, we deny the blazing colors of the wild God in our world and assume that the drab grays of our own invention are all the colors there are. When we are lazy, we deny the vitality of the opportunities before us. When we hunt for excuses, we deny the obligations under which God has given us to live. When we harbor grudges, we deny that God's mercy makes all things new in each pulse of time. When we resent others their successes, we deny that God gives each of us our own story, not the stories of others. When we hurt others because of our own selfishness, we deny that God loves us with such sufficiency that selfishness is idolatry. When we sink into greed and gluttony, we deny that in God we possess and enjoy all things.

Hurt, neglect, sleepwalking, inattention, laziness, excuses, grudges, resentment, selfishness, greed, and gluttony add up to a monstrous denial of the most real thing in our lives, that God is our intimate creator and lover. The weight of that denial harms others, blinds us to God, and blights our lives like a plague of locusts. And sometimes we do not even notice. In the face of all this, Lent calls us to observe Joel's call: "Yet even now, says the Lord, / return to me with all your heart, / with fasting, with weeping, and with mourning; / rend your hearts and not your clothing."

Lent calls us to give up the denial and turn to God. Although it is difficult to turn in all those dimensions of sin, each of which clutches at us like devouring locusts, we have the grace of God to do so, and this season to set our goals. The power of the Creator is ready with renewal. Listen again to Paul:

> As we work together with him, we urge you also not to accept the grace of God in vain. For he says, "At an acceptable time I have listened to you, and on a day of salvation I have helped you." See, now is the acceptable time; see, now is the day of salvation! We are putting no obstacle in anyone's way, so that no fault may be found with our ministry, but as servants of God we have commended ourselves in every way: through great endurance, in afflictions, hardships, calamities, beatings, imprisonments, riots, labors, sleepless nights, hunger; by purity, knowledge, patience, kindness, holiness of spirit, genuine love, truthful speech, and the power of God; with the weapons of righteousness for the right hand and for the left, in honor and dishonor, in ill repute and good repute. We are treated as impostors, and yet are true; as unknown, and yet are well known; as dying, and see—we are alive; as punished, and yet not killed; as sorrowful, yet always rejoicing; as poor, yet making many rich, as having nothing, and yet possessing everything.

Brothers and sisters, that is the way to live. Come bear the mark of the return to God and the vitality of creation. Amen.

20

Temptation[1]

Genesis 2:11–17; 3: 1–7; Romans 5:11–19; Matthew 4:1–11

For those of us who shape our Christian lives somewhat by the liturgical calendar, the move from Transfiguration Sunday, whose astonishing transfiguring experiences we celebrated last week, to the first Sunday of the Lenten penitential season might seem a rough jolt. Yet I think it is not so. The question that remained at the end of our consideration of transfiguring experiences was how to tell the destructive, death-dealing ones from those that engage God in ways that lead to or enhance salvation. The answer I sketched briefly last week was that the transfiguring experiences, however weird, need to be set in an interpretive context in which they can be seen to engage God in a true way. The experiences do not interpret themselves. By themselves they might be bizarre and meaningless; they might be destructive hallucinations. But grasped within the context of a richly lived Christian life, they can be instruments for engaging God more deeply.

Suppose you are very poor, near to starving and you fear you are indeed starving. You begin to hallucinate. The recurrent hallucination is that the devil comes to you and tells you that you are the omnipotent Child of God and that all you have to do is command the stones and they will become bread. This hallucination becomes an obsession every day your efforts to find food reach the eleventh hour. So in weak desperation you go to your spiritual advisor for help. (Everyone has a spiritual advisor, I trust.)

1. Preached February 13, 2005, the, first Sunday of Lent.

Your advisor asks you whether you are indeed the Child of God, as your hallucination says, and you answer cynically, "How could I be so hungry if I were?"

"But are you the Child of God?"

"Well, the Bible says I am," you say.

"If you could change the stones to bread," the advisor asks, "would you?"

"Oh, dear God yes," you mutter.

"Does being the Child of God mean you have miraculous powers?"

"No," you say, "there is nothing special about my powers."

"Then what does it mean that you are the Child of God?" the advisor asks.

"The Bible says that God's entire creation is for the benefit of God's children," you answer.

"So then," the advisor says, "have you been to the soup kitchen to eat? Have you gone to the shelters to sleep? Have you gone to social services for welfare? Have you applied for medical benefits? Have you gotten job training? Why are you starving in the midst of all these?"

Now you confess with understanding, "This vision of magical powers to turn stones to bread tempted me to a grandiose pride that turned me away from God's plenty and support all around me. I succumbed to the temptation to believe that as a Child of God I am supposed to be God, though I would have fed only myself. Now I understand and am so sorry."

Your spiritual advisor says, "One does not live by bread alone, but by every word that comes from the mouth of God. You are forgiven. Now seek out your God's graces."

The spiritual advisor transported the transfiguring vision of the temptation to grandiose powers of turning stones to bread into the larger context of divine grace. In that interpretive context the vision heals the disengagement from God and opens us to the plenty around us. The people whose starvation cannot be avoided because there are no soup kitchens, sleeping shelters, welfare systems, medical aid, and job training, suffer from our failure to do God's obvious work.

Suppose that you are a sincere and faithful Christian, but a risk taker. Suppose you are a student who believes that God won't let you fail and so play too much rather than study enough. The reason for your belief is a transfiguring cartoon fantasy of God's angels on your shoulders to give you the inspired answers on the test. (Perhaps this was prompted by some television shows?) Or suppose you are in business and see a great opportunity that also entails the possibility of losing everything; buoyed by a vision of God's angels protecting his own, without counting the cost you leap at the opportunity, daring God to let you fail. And you fail. In despair at flunking out or losing your entire fortune, you go to your spiritual advisor and say, "Jesus! Where was God when I needed him?"

The advisor asks, "Wasn't it your responsibility to study for the exams? Wasn't it your responsibility to calculate how much you would be willing to lose for the possibility of gaining the business advantage?"

"Yes," you say, "but how can God let his faithful servants be so destroyed?"

"Why do you put God to the test?" asks the advisor. "Do you think God to be so small that you can manipulate providence to your advantage? Is God not the creator of the other students who study much harder and the other business people in the competition?"

So you confess that you are selfish in wanting the vast impersonal processes of creation to be bent to your own ends.

"No, not only that," responds the advisor, "you need to confess your lack of faith that makes you always put God to the test. You need to confess that you do not have faith to engage the actual world God gives you, with precisely the tests and opportunities of your life. You need to confess that, in putting God to the test, you have been fleeing from the actual life God gives you in which you might not always be a winner and come out on top, in which all you can do is try your best. Why put God to the test when it is you whom God has under examination?"

"Yes, I see," you say. "Jesus, help me live my life"

The transfiguring vision of divine protection, which so many of us have in various forms, tempts us to avoid life and belligerently reject the God who gives us that life. But interpreted precisely as a temptation, that vision stokes the faith and courage to accept even broken and bedraggled lives with gratitude to God.

Suppose you are a political leader of a powerful country and are deeply committed to bringing world peace, establishing universal justice, eradicating hunger, and installing democracy in every nation. Then you have a transfiguring vision that you can impose these goals if you devote yourself to the acquisition of dominating power and wealth. It is not enough to try your best with the resources at hand, because God knows people can undermine peace, subvert justice, starve others to fulfill their own greed, and use government to enrich their own pockets. Your pursuit of dominating power and wealth to do good becomes an infinite passion because you never have enough. Any bombs that are not yours can be used against you; any competitive centers of wealth can buy off your success. Though you sell your soul to the sword and the dollar, the Lord of those earthly powers turns up as the god of chaos, and you are mired in unwinnable wars in a global economy that outsources your resources. "Lord Jesus!" you cry, "I was trying so hard to establish your kingdom! Why won't the lion lie down with that... lamb!"

"My friend," your spiritual advisor says, "it is God who makes lions and lambs. God's people often think they have to fight about things in order to get justice for themselves; one people's hunger leads to violence that starves others worse; and no one trusts democracy if they think there is a chance they can get dominating power and wealth by themselves. Are you not the villain here?"

"But Lord," you say, "I have sacrificed my allies, my honor, my self-respect, and my sense of due measure in order to acquire the power to control things for the good. I cannot stop worshiping the promise of power, and I hate that, and myself."

"My friend," says Jesus, "worship the Lord your God, and serve only him."

"How can I break the hold of the promise of power to worship God," you plead, "without allowing the possibility of more violence, injustice, hunger and tyranny? I'm holding back the sea with my hand in the dike as it is! And I hate what I've become too much to ask for the pardon to worship God."

"You do not have to merit pardon to worship God," says the Lord. "The ever-creating love that courses through those whom you think you need to control runs in your veins too. Your temptation is not really to the chaotic sources of possible power, as you believe, but to bondage to that possible power. You need the bondage. You tell yourself you want to control things for the good: but in fact you are terrified of control that can never be perfect, and want to escape responsibility, and flee to the excuse of Satan's bondage. Give it up! Just do the best you can. Respect God's dignity in all the others. And worship the God who creates you more than able always to make worship of God a possibility for your infinite passion. Repent and do it!"

"Thank you, Lord Jesus," you say.

Temptation

Temptation exposed to the context of God leads not to fall but to God.

Suppose you and your beloved are strolling in a garden when, with a blinding flash, a very skinny theologian approaches you and says, "Faust, let me tempt you with this fruit. The old wives' tale is that it is poison, but millions of people have eaten it for thousands of years and lived to tell the tale. Those who eat it learn God's ways to tell the right from wrong. And see how beautiful it is!"

Your beloved, who is a better theologian, replies, "You clever angel of dark light, you can't trick us out of gratitude to God and obedience to creation's givens for us. We've tasted that fruit time and again. The first time it tasted like life-giving food, and we forgot the source of true nourishment. The first time our new wisdom about right and wrong brought only shame, and we forgot it was God's wisdom. The first time it was beautiful and delicious by itself, and we forgot what beauty truly signifies. Forgetting whence we came, and where we were, and what things ultimately signify, we found ourselves left with only a greater hunger, a shameful self-consciousness, and a beauty that was only a reflection of ourselves. Over time, however, with much pain and sacrifice, we have come to see that the fruit is forbidden only when we forget the God who placed it in the garden. Through many hard lessons, and repeated revelations through our fog, we have come to see the fruit as a sign of God's loving nurture, God's obliging tasks for us, and God's beauty more glorious than a natural polish. So, we'll take the fruit, and thank you for it."

"You'll what?" says Satan. "This temptation will make you mine, not God's!"

"Oh, no," you say. "My beloved showed me that a love willing to go to death for love's sake transfigures temptations into testimonies to divinity. Your trials are our spiritual exercises. Your temptations lead to our freedom. Your fruit's alluring beauty reflects God's glory. Share your fruit with us; it is so beautiful."

"Damn!" cries Satan.

"Come with us," say you and your beloved in unison.

Lent's lesson is that God's redeeming power is so great that even the fiercest evil forces can be transfigured to reflect God's glory in justice and mercy. Good things can be transfigured to reveal God when we see them in the context of our approach to God. Bad things can be transfigured the same way. But it is so much harder to engage God with bad things than good things that we need the sweat of Lent to work things through. The temptations of grandiose fantasies of power, of obsessive demands to be loved, and of passions for dominance fueled by self-hate are fiendishly difficult to transfigure into humility and love before our divine beloved. With the companionship of Jesus, however, our Lenten discipline can do that work. I invite you into that grand transfiguration in which the world is made holy. Amen.

21

The Difference Faith Makes[1]

Genesis 12:1–4a; Romans 4:1–5, 11–17; John 3:17

We live in two worlds, according to the New Testament. One is the world of ordinary life, with concerns and values of which the New Testament sometimes takes a dim view. The other is God's world, which includes the ordinary world but sets it in a context of spiritual meaning usually missing from ordinary life. Jesus sometimes likened the ordinary world to a kind of half sleep from which we should be awakened to see that God's world is at hand. We access the ordinary world through the customs of thinking and acting. We access God's world through faith expressed in insider Christian symbols. That is the difference faith makes, gaining some limited access to God's version of our world.

Our gospel reading today is an example of appealing to special insider knowledge, for which John the Evangelist is famous. His early readers who were thoroughly familiar with the Hebrew Bible would hear a variety of symbolic references in this passage. For instance, they would have known what to make of the reference to Moses lifting up the serpent in the wilderness. The twenty-first chapter of Numbers tells how the Israelites on the exodus were moping along through the wilderness complaining, as usual, about God's deficient food and beverage service. So God, not to be messed with, sends poisonous snakes among them, biting the people and killing many. The leaders complain to Moses and God tells him to make a bronze

1. Preached February 20, 2005, the second Sunday in Lent.

image of a serpent and lift it up on a pole. An Israelite who has been bitten by a poisonous snake can look at the serpent on the pole, God says, and be saved from death. That was actually a bit of Egyptian magic. The snake on a pole has come down to us as a symbol of the medical profession, and you frequently see the sign of one or two snakes crawling to the top of a pole on the side of an ambulance. John uses that symbol as an emblem of Jesus lifted up on a cross: as the Israelites could be saved from the bite of the serpent by looking up at the snake on the pole, so we can be saved by looking up to the crucified Christ.

Our text from John's Gospel is especially rich in biblical symbolism that you get if you are a biblical insider. But John has a double layer of insider knowledge in the text, in this passage and throughout the gospel. He writes of Jesus talking with his contemporary, Nicodemus, and yet John has Jesus make references that only John's own audience would understand seventy years or more after the events. The reference to Jesus being lifted up on the cross is a case in point; only those who knew about Jesus's crucifixion, subsequent to his conversation with Nicodemus, would understand the reference to Moses lifting up the serpent in the wilderness. John was writing for his own community who knew the story of Jesus and also John's interpretation of it.

Consider poor Nicodemus. He was a Pharisee, and John uses that as an identification of respect for the piety of Pharisees. Nicodemus was also a "leader of the Jews," which means he was a member of the Sanhedrin, the body of ruling Jews responsible to the Roman occupation forces. Nicodemus, you remember, was one of those along with Joseph of Arimathea who later took care of Jesus's body after the crucifixion. In the story in our text, Nicodemus sneaks to Jesus by night to say that Jesus must really come from God if he is able to do the signs he does. Jesus answers, "No one can see the kingdom of God without being born from above." Then silly Nicodemus asks, "How can anyone be born after having grown old? Can one enter a second time into the mother's womb and be born?" At this point John's readers must be rolling in the pews in laughter because of this literal mindedness. Of course they knew about spiritual rebirth, a function of existing self-consciously in God's world. Being reborn is only a metaphor for that, though a very powerful one. They knew about new life in Christ, and could laugh at Nicodemus' ignorance.

This kind of speech with double meaning, one meaning for the ordinary people to whom the speech was given, another for those in the community of the Gospel, runs throughout John's Gospel. Think of the passage from chapter 6 where Jesus says, "I am the living bread that came down from heaven. Whoever eats of this bread will live forever; and the bread that I will give for the life of the world is my flesh." John writes, "The Jews then disputed among themselves, saying, 'How can this man give us his flesh to eat?'"—literalists like Nicodemus. Jesus goes on, "Very truly, I tell you, unless you eat the flesh of the Son of Man and drink his blood, you have no life in you. Those who eat my flesh and drink my blood have eternal life. . ." John's readers recognize a reference to the Eucharist, but Jesus's hearers thought he was outrageously advocating cannibalism with himself as dinner.

John's literary device of double meaning, one for the people in the event, another for his readers who understand, is not *mere* literary device. By its very form it signifies that we are born into a world in which spiritual things do not make much sense, such as climbing into a mother's womb to be born again, or eating the quadriceps of your teacher. But then when you have the higher knowledge, as John's own readership community supposedly did, the spiritual matters all make sense. John's point is that the community with the spiritual knowledge is the community of salvation, and it is the community of faith. More exactly, John wanted his readers to know that there is a level of spiritual understanding to which they could aspire if they did not have it. We are John's readers with precisely that challenge.

How do we get into that community, or become it, so that the matters of the spirit make sense to us? Like Abram, we are called to go from the country of our birth on a pilgrimage into a foreign land, the spiritual land. John's image for this call, of course, is not a journey but a rebirth. "No one can enter the kingdom of God without being born of water and Spirit." The word for "Spirit" also means "wind" and "breath." What does it mean to be born of the Spirit? How can we be moved by the wind of God, which blows where it chooses? How can our breath become the breath of God? Obviously it is not an obstetrical event, as poor Nicodemus thought.

Nor is the rebirth to be identified with certain signs of the Spirit such as powerful emotional experiences, speaking in tongues, or the like, although these signs have been taken from biblical times down to our own as indications that one is being wrenched from one birth to another, from one country to the promised land. Rather, the rebirth means that we have to be remade in our fundamental families and personalities. We have to become new people, said Jesus in John's Gospel, in order to understand about heavenly things.

How do we become new people? The temptation is to think that the transformation is made by our moral commitments and achievements. Morality is certainly central to both the Hebrew Bible and the New Testament. Yet morality in the rich biblical sense of righteousness before God is not the means but the result of being in the new country, the result of rebirth, the result of belonging to the community that grasps spiritual matters. Paul's point in the epistle for today is that Abram was accounted truly righteous by God before he had done anything of significant moral righteousness. Rather, Abram was approved because of his faith in God's call to risk everything for the promise of the new country.

Faith is what makes the difference between the old country and the new, the old life and the new. In our texts, faith is like looking up to the saving serpent on the pole, like looking to the Son of Man lifted up, "so that whoever believes in him may have eternal life." Faith is believing that "God so loved the world that he gave his only Son, so that everyone who believes in him may not perish but may have eternal life." Eternal life here does not mean immortality or an afterlife, although John (and Jesus) did believe in that too. Eternal life means rather a contemporary participation in the divine life that does not perish. Although our personal bodies perish in time, God's life in which we participate through the Holy Spirit does not perish. Our participation in the divine life consists in living in the Holy Spirit.

Our last question, then, is in what the divine life in the Holy Spirit consists. The answer here is very clear from the rest of John's Gospel, as well as his letters. The divine life is love, and we participate in that insofar as we participate in communities of love. In Jesus's so-called Farewell Discourses in John 11–17, he makes clear that the disciples are to live under a new commandment to love one another. They can do this because he has already loved them, and they have responded by loving him. Moreover, Jesus has extended himself to them in love because God the Father has loved him and he has loved the Father.

For all its beauty, Jesus's love for his disciples brings him misunderstanding, betrayal, and ultimately death. Yet the love was worth it. The disciples too will find that loving one another is not always a matter of positive reinforcement. Sometimes love leads to crucifixion.

So faith is the commitment to give ourselves to the life of love, with all the rejections, incomprehension, hurts, and possibly ultimate failures love can involve. Love is never finished. It always is a matter of staying true to the promise. Love is not like arriving in a new country and settling there.

The Difference Faith Makes

It is rather like Abraham's constant search, never finished, for the promised land. Faith in the God of love is not investment in an experiment that within our lives might prove itself to be the successful way to go. On the contrary, love always runs the risk of going sour. Yet the only thing that carries love through the sour periods is the faith to stick with it, the faith to bear its crosses. This does not mean that we should stay in destructive relationships because we are supposed to love the person to whom we are related destructively. No, genuinely to love a person in a destructive relationship is to get out of that relationship. But love does mean to remain vulnerable to love's rejection. To become a lover who remains vulnerable and faithful in that vulnerability is to become a new person.

The old life teaches us to seek our advantage, cultivating those loves that are to our advantage. To be reborn means to take on a life of love that can endure failure and that perseveres in building the institutions of community that embody justice, piety, faith, and hope even when those institutions are ready to be beaten down.

The faith to commit ourselves to the life of love so astonishingly taught and exemplified by Jesus makes all the difference in the world. It is like setting out for a new country in response to God's call. It is like being reborn in the water of baptism that frees us from our sins and enrolls us in the new community of love. It is like being reborn in the Spirit of God that breathes through us as we engage the issues of our time, our sorry politics, our dysfunctional families, our mixed-up souls, all to subject them to the humility and discipline of love.

I invite you to faithful commitment to the loving way of Jesus. With faith, we leave behind the bondage of ignorance in spiritual matters, the bondage of neediness for idolatrous power, and the bondage of the old life of the search for self-advantage. With faith, we gain the new life in which God's spirit of love lifts us into God's eternal life at the very same time that we risk ourselves in love at the right hand and at the left. Nicodemus might have been a little silly in his question whether he had to enter his mother's womb to be born again. But he learned Jesus's lesson. Remember it was he who, with Joseph of Arimathea, persevered in love of Jesus after the crucifixion and took his body to ready it for the resurrection. May our Lenten disciplines increase our faith to persevere for the newborn life of love. Amen.

22

Seeing beyond Expectations[1]

1 Samuel 16:1–13; Ephesians 5:1–14; John 9:1–41

Some people say that "seeing is believing," by which they mean that the testimony of the senses is far better than hearsay, or even than reasoning that is subject to error. Our texts from 1 Samuel and John, however, suggest that we ordinarily see what we already believe, that our sight is guided by our expectations. Genuine sight needs to get beneath the appearances governed by our expectations.

In the case of Samuel's search for someone to anoint as the new king of Israel, everyone expected him to pick Jesse's first son, Eliab, because he was big and strong, rather like King Saul, the first anointed king who subsequently had been rejected by God. But God said to Samuel about Eliab, "Do not look on his appearance or on the height of his stature, because I have rejected him; for the Lord does not see as mortals see; they look on the outward appearance, but the LORD looks on the heart." We look on the outward appearance, but God looks on the heart. How true! At the Lord's urging, Samuel rejected all the other sons of Jesse, save the last and least, David, who had been left to tend the flocks. Samuel anointed David to be the next king; the word for the anointed one in this sense was the Hebrew cognate of "messiah." King Saul was the first "messiah," for he too had been anointed. But David better fulfilled the ideal of the kingly messiah, uniting Israel after Saul's death, defeating its enemies, and extending its territory to

---

1. Preached March 6, 2005, the fourth Sunday of Lent.

its greatest extent; he was a mighty warrior and a brilliant strategist, defeating both external enemies and armed rebellions among his own people. In Jesus's time, the Pharisees and others hoped for another messiah on the model of David, someone who would drive out the Romans and reestablish the power of the Israelite or Jewish nation. Jesus obviously was not that kind of person, and so was rejected by those who hoped for another David.

Before leaving the story of David, however, it is worthwhile to recall that he was a complex character. Although ultimately uniting the twelve tribes of Israel and giving identity to a unified nation, David early had a falling out with King Saul and formed his own mercenary army to work for the Philistines for a while. With that army he conquered Jerusalem, which belonged to a Canaanite people called the Jebusites. That is why Jerusalem is called the "City of David," because he conquered it with his private army, not with a levy of warriors from the twelve tribes of Israel like the army of Saul. This made Jerusalem a good neutral capital, not a town owned by any of the tribes, though it was in the territory of David's own tribe, Judah. As an individual, David was a sexual predator, sending Bathsheba's husband to his death so that she might be his. David's family was filled with intrigue, with his wives and sons plotting against one another to determine his successor. His children were involved in rape and incest, as well as outright rebellion in the case of Absalom whom David loved dearly. David was a complex, deeply flawed human being, just as we are, only with kingly proportions. His greatest virtue, however, was that he danced before the Lord, both literally and figuratively. When he sinned, he repented. When he made mistakes, he sought the Lord. When he won battles, he credited God. When he governed the state, he did it for God. What he learned in his long life he learned from living before the Lord. Despite all his mistakes and sins, he died with a wise son to succeed him and a healthy kingdom to pass on. Who would have seen this God-intoxicated world-beater, this voracious consumer of life's loves and opportunities, looking at young David standing before Samuel, ruddy, with beautiful eyes, and handsome, almost a feminine creature in comparison with his brothers? Only someone who could see beyond the expectations of appearances into the heart.

John's story of Jesus and the blind man is a far more complex case of seeing beyond expectations. John has an elaborate theme of visibility and invisibility, sight and blindness. As Jesus and his disciples were walking along, they encountered the blind beggar. The disciples asked whether the man was born blind because of his own sin or because of that of his parents.

The connection of blindness to sin has a powerfully ironic twist at the end of the story when Jesus said "'I came into this world for judgment so that those who do not see may see, and those who do see may become blind.' Some of the Pharisees near him heard this and said to him, 'Surely we are not blind, are we?' Jesus said to them, 'If you were blind, you would not have sin. But now that you say, "we see," your sin remains.'" In other words, if they had not claimed understanding, they would not be accountable for sin.

In response to the disciples' question about who was responsible for the beggar's blindness, Jesus denied that any one was responsible. But he did say that the man's blindness had a purpose, namely, to set Jesus up for an important public miracle, demonstrating the work of God. Now you and I might not approve of this conception of a God who makes a man suffer blindness from birth to adulthood just to demonstrate Jesus's divine powers. We do not believe that illness has a purpose, for punishment or anything else, although of course we can give meaning to illness. At any rate, Jesus gave the blind man sight, without even being asked to do so, by the way. The man's neighbors were incredulous. The Pharisees asked how he had been healed, and the formerly blind man gave them just the facts: he put mud on my eyes, and washed, and I could see. When asked where Jesus was, the man said simply that he didn't know, which was true.

The Pharisees then got into a theological wrangle. One side said that Jesus must be a sinner because he worked on the Sabbath, while the other side said that he could not do such miraculous healings unless he were from God. Then, strangely, they asked the formerly blind man what he thought about Jesus, strange because the man had been blind all his life and worked only as a beggar, not a likely theological consultant. The man said Jesus was a prophet because of his power to heal. Not believing in miraculous healings, the Pharisees then decided that the man could not have been blind previously. But his parents confirmed that he had been. The parents, however, expected to be thrown out of the temple community for not agreeing with the Pharisees, so they sent them back to talk with their son. When the Pharisees told him that Jesus must be a sinner, the man said he didn't know about that. What he did know was that he had been blind and Jesus gave him sight. When the Pharisees annoyed the man, he suggested wryly that they must want to be Jesus's disciples because they kept questioning him about Jesus. He then said that, if they were right about God listening only to the righteous, then Jesus the healer must be from God.

Seeing beyond Expectations

Both the Pharisees and the man's parents were blinded by their expectations, the former by their theological expectations, the latter by expectations of retribution from the Pharisees. Even Jesus was a bit callous toward the blind man by treating him as an occasion for a revelatory miracle, although when he heard that the Pharisees expelled the formerly blind man from the temple he sought the man out and declared his identity as the Son of Man or Messiah. Jesus gave the man not only sight but a new home when both the temple and his parents failed him.

The one person in this story who had perfect sight was the blind man. He knew who he was, a blind beggar, and had no expectations. He accepted Jesus's gift of sight with gratitude, and told the story of it with no embellishments. Unlike his parents, he saw through the confused and hypocritical Pharisees with fearless steadiness and irony. He learned who Jesus was only when Jesus told him, not from any religious expectation, although he always understood his healing to have been divinely caused. When he realized who Jesus was, he worshiped him.

Would we not be blessed to have the sight of the blind man! With no ego expectations of grandiose righteousness or self-excusing victimization, we would know just who we are without illusions. We could accept the demeaning status of having to beg without being demeaned by it. We could accept sudden and unexpected blessings, such as serious healing, with gratitude and equanimity. We could tell others the truth, saying what we know and admitting what we do not know, without having to embellish the truth with hopes and disappointments. We could take the consequences of the truth without fear, knowing that whatever is comes from God. Best of all, we would not hate God because of the pain in our lives and we would not love God because of the good in our lives. Rather, with the blind man's sight, with his ascetic lack of expectations, we would love God for God's own sake when we meet him. We would delight to discover that the person who heals our disabilities and dispenses grace is also the Son of God. We would see through to God as found in the least of our brothers and sisters.

My friends, I know that it is customary to see God primarily in terms of what God can do to us or for us. Fear of divine wrath on the one hand and hope in divine promises on the other are the doorways of most religious views, if not the substance of most religion itself. Yet those are only appearances, too human ways of seeing, because they really are about us, projections of our fears and desires, rather than about God. Like God, we should strive to see beyond the appearances into the heart of individuals, human affairs, and God. We might see beyond the handsome, ruddy boy with beautiful eyes to the soul of a hero of humanity. We might see beyond the hypocritical intrigues about religious righteousness to the humility of true repentance and gratitude. And we might see beyond God "for us" to the true God to whom the only real response is worship. Amen.

23

Spirit and Flesh[1]

Ezekiel 37:1–14; Romans 8:1–11; John 11:1–45

The three texts of our Scripture today have given rise to three different, and perhaps problematic, theologies of the relation of spirit to flesh. We are fleshly people, evolving in nature with needs and appetites that fuel human society. Yet we are spiritual people in our relation to God. If we are not well-related to God, our spiritual lives are poor. Ideally, our spirit is supposed to be infused with God's spirit. In fact, the most fundamental theme of Christian redemption is that the Word of God takes on human flesh and walks among us. We do not have to go to God. God is incarnate in and among us. The Christian approach to spirit is not to find it above life or in the by-and-by, but in the very flesh of life. Yet Christian incarnationalism is difficult to grasp and, when grasped, it is still difficult to swallow.

The dry bones text from Ezekiel is one of the most vivid images in the whole Bible. One of my earliest memories is of a men's quartet in my church in Saint Louis singing, "Them bones, them bones, them dry bones." The connection of the thigh bone to the hip bone was my first conscious awareness that human anatomy is more than skin deep. Imagine Ezekiel surveying that ancient battlefield of dry bones and calling upon them to come together with a great rattle, then grow sinews, muscles, and skin. But they were only bodies, like the doll God made out of mud according to Genesis 2. God had to breathe his breath, or spirit, into Adam to make him

1. Preached March 13, 2005, the fifth Sunday of Lent.

a living creature. God tells Ezekiel to call in the divine breath to give living spirit to the army of newly enfleshed dead men. When the divine wind comes at his call, the people come to life.

The point of Ezekiel's text, however, was not a parable about God breathing life into otherwise inanimate bodies, as in the Genesis account. Rather, his point was that Israel had been defeated and scattered in exile like a beaten army, and that God would recall Israel home. Ezekiel was rather harsh in his reasons for Israel's defeat: they had to do with Israel abandoning God and pursuing sin and idolatry. God was behind their defeat. But God would also redeem them as a people and bring them back to the promised land. In Ezekiel's text, God does not directly reassemble the bones and breathe life into them; rather, he has Ezekiel cause all this by "prophesying." I suspect that Ezekiel saw a significant role for prophets such as himself in the redemption and reestablishment of Israel.

We Americans today might not identify much with ancient Israel's sorry state, for we are still the nation that dictates to others. Many of us believe, however, that Ezekiel's indictment of Israel might have some application to us. Where is our godly commitment to peacemaking, to putting the poor and oppressed first, to policies that heal those afflicted with diseases such as AIDS, to feeding the hungry, clothing the naked, and freeing the prisoners? Why do we make war out of anger, set our foreign and domestic policies to feed the greed of the rich, and back away from multilateral treaties that would require some restraint from us to protect the environment and establish international law? Where did we get the idolatrous idea that we should impose our political polities on people who do not choose them? Ezekiel sounds a warning to which we should listen. He also promises hope that, no matter how far we fall, and how much we suffer the consequences of greedy belligerence, God can redeem the nation. Those who despair should remember that the bones did come together, grow flesh, and receive the divine breath of life.

Paul's text tells a darker story. For him the term "flesh" did not symbolize God's creation, which was pronounced good. For Paul, "flesh" symbolized a commitment to sensuality, especially sexuality, that fails to put sensual impulses in their places. He probably recognized that sex in its place is good, although he did not say that. Acquisition of wealth is good if distributed with charity. Eating and drinking are good if not done to excess. The flesh is good if infused with the spirit. In Paul's rather dour worldview, however, sex, productive work, eating and drinking, and other ordinary

Spirit and Flesh

functions of life typically become addictions. He frequently characterized sin as bondage, as addictions are matters of bondage. He pictured human beings as so addicted to the things that otherwise are healthy needs and purposes that they lose their health and become ends in themselves, binding us in slavery to sin. Recent theologians often fault Paul for denying the goodness of creation by harping on how human beings have distorted it. Because of Paul, the Christian tradition has little good to say about sex except for its utilitarian function of reproduction, little good to say about marriage except that it can keep you out of adultery, and little good to say about enjoying life except as a foretaste of a better life to come. Paul looked for a quick ending of the present age and a flight from it to be with Jesus, without much attention to the redemption of the flesh in this life. We can fault his theology of creation, perhaps.

But was he not right in so much of what he said about our bondage to the flesh? And did he not say also in our passage that, "If the Spirit of him who raised Jesus from the dead dwells in you, he who raised Christ from the dead will give life to your mortal bodies also through his Spirit that dwells in you"? Paul did proclaim the incarnation even if he was reluctant to say much about how the indwelling Spirit of God might improve our mortal bodies of flesh.

John's gospel is the opposite of Paul's in this respect. For John, Jesus was all about the loveliness of the flesh, of this life. To be sure, there is a high symbolic structure to John's Gospel. The raising of Lazarus is the last and most spectacular of the miracles that Jesus performed, beginning with the simple, almost frivolous one of making wine out of water at the wedding in Cana. The miracles all were to show the power of God to be manifest in the world in ways most people missed. Jesus's own resurrection was the crowning demonstration of the Lordship of God within the world. The raising of Lazarus was also the incident that set the government and temple authorities out to get Jesus. But pay attention to the loving details of the story.

The story begins by establishing that Jesus loved Lazarus as a friend, along with his sisters Mary and Martha; the other Gospels never indicate that Jesus had friends, only disciples. The other miracle healing stories all have to do with first encounters, not with a preexisting love. Then the story says that the sisters sent to Jesus who was in hiding because his enemies had tried to stone him. Jesus's felt their need of him but with great reluctance stayed back so that sick Lazarus would die before he can go perform a miraculous healing. Jesus apparently wanted him to die so that he could raise someone from the dead, not just cure an illness. Notice Jesus's intense dialogue with his disciples about all this, especially with Thomas. When Jesus finally came to Bethany, Lazarus had been in the tomb four days; folk religion of the time believed that souls of the dead stayed near the body for about four days and then left, meaning that after four days Lazarus was as dead as dead can be. Friends of the family from Jerusalem were consoling the sisters.

As he approached, Martha ran to meet Jesus with a somewhat incoherent speech about how he could have helped if he had been there earlier. Jesus told her that Lazarus would live again, which she interpreted to mean that he would rise at the last general resurrection. Jesus replied that he himself, there in the flesh, was the resurrection. Martha, better at managing things than at theology, ran back for Mary, the contemplative one. Mary fell down at Jesus's feet in worship and said Lazarus would not have died if Jesus had been there. At this point, Jesus's high resolution to let Lazarus die so he could demonstrate divine power wavered. He broke down when he saw the sisters' grief, and that of the mourners. "See how he loved him," said the people.

When the group arrived at the tomb, Jesus broke down again. And then he called Lazarus, whose body was in a state of decay, to come out of the tomb, to come back to them, to live again. This was not a fancy resurrection to a celestial body, as Paul imagined it in Corinthians. This was a call back to the flesh. It demonstrated God's power, but not for a general resurrection of the dead. It demonstrated God's power to bring Lazarus back to this life. Lazarus was deeply loved, by Jesus, his sisters, and the crowd. And they wanted him amongst them again.

John's Gospel is startling with its complicated theological representations of the drama of divine power, of Jesus's sometimes outrageous claims about himself, and its apparent approval of using people's suffering to demonstrate divine power. Yet the genius of the gospel is that it illustrates those things with the intimacy of personal love. John's Jesus had a social life; his conversations are recorded as well as his speeches. Jesus weeping over Jerusalem in the other Gospels was a symbolic act. Weeping over Lazarus was the squeezing of his heart. John says that the power of resurrection came to a man who broke down at the pain caused by what he had to do. The mighty power of God's spirit dwelt in a man whose flesh loved, laughed, grieved, and wept.

The lesson for us is not that we should go out and attempt miracles. Rather we should love, laugh, grieve, and weep. We should not buffer ourselves against human contact. We should not pass up opportunities to enjoy friends and celebrate life's moments. We should not fail to cultivate family and friendships, entering emotionally into all their affairs. We should not fail to bear one another's burdens. We should not protect ourselves from grief. We should not hold back tears or protect our hearts from being broken. For it is in the intensity of open, loving, intimate personal life that we can receive God's spirit and be truly spiritual people.

God's spirit is not something blown into us from the outside, as Ezekiel might have thought. Our flesh with its loving, weepy sensuality should not be suppressed until covered by the Spirit, as Paul might have thought. By making our flesh supple, full, porous, and open to life's intimacies we welcome the Spirit of God and can live intensely as we were created to be in fleshly form before God our creator, judge, and lover.

In John's Gospel, Jesus insists that his great work has been to make his disciples friends with one another and with him, and through him with God. He instructs them with his new commandment, to love one another as he has loved them. We Christians are still obligated by that commandment, to love with the fullness of incarnation. When we do that, we bear God's Spirit and have our own true spiritual nature.

Moreover, I am pleased to tell you, friends, that when we engage life with divinely passionate love, miracles do happen. We might not make wine from water without benefit of grapes, but we can make bounties happen for the humble of the earth. We might not cure the blind by putting mud on their eyes, but we can cure them many other ways. We might not raise the long-dead but we can prevent many deaths and with sufficient love keep the memory of the dead alive for those to whom they are bound in heart. With love we can open the eyes of the spiritually blind. With love we can comfort the oppressed and dismantle their oppression. With love we can make peace where others would make war. With love we can feed the hungry and cloth the naked. With love we can break the bonds of sin and open the doors of the prisons so that all might be free. With love we can gather the people exiled in alienation and unite them as loving friends. The flesh of loving intimacy among friends is the perfect vehicle for God's Spirit.

My friends, let our prayer be that we inhabit our own flesh with such vigor and gratitude that it becomes the natural dwelling place of God's spirit in all we are and do. Amen.

24

The Power of Humility[1]

Isaiah 50:1–9a; Philippians 2:1–11; Matthew 27:11–54

Palm Sunday is commonly represented as a triumphal entry of Jesus into Jerusalem, riding on a donkey, which was the ceremonial act of a king. The crowd hailed Jesus as the Son of David, saying "Blessed is the one who comes in the name of the Lord." The familiar story is told in the twenty-first chapter of Matthew, verses 1–11. We know that the crowd was hoping for a messiah as David has been, a king with the military skill and power to deliver Israel from the Romans.

We have seen a great deal of triumphalist thinking in recent politics. America's government has cast the country into the messianic role of saving the world for democracy. But America's messianic self-understanding is not that of a teaching messiah like Jesus. It is more that of a fighting messiah like David who conquered a lot of territory in his time, or like Cyrus the Great of Persia who conquered a great deal more territory and was called messiah because he sent the Jews back to Jerusalem from their exile. The American messianic mission has led us to conquer Afghanistan and Iraq whose former governments opposed our democratizing plans for them. We've threatened Iran and North Korea, whom our president has linked with Iraq as the "Axis of Evil," and seem surprised when they want to develop nuclear weapons to keep America at bay. Our government is convinced that it can triumph over any country that stands in its way.

1. Preached March 20, 2005, Palm Sunday.

Jesus's triumph, of course, was very short-lived. He offered no armed resistance to the Romans, nor did he collect any army as David had. After his Palm Sunday entry into Jerusalem he spent the next four days teaching, mainly in the temple, and going each night back to the suburb of Bethany, most likely to stay with Mary, Martha, and Lazarus.

What Jesus taught in those days, according to Matthew, had little or nothing to do with politics, the Roman occupation, or insurrection. In fact, that was the time he said to render to Caesar the things that are Caesar's and to God the things that are God's. Jesus teaching was occupied with God, though with a special twist. His teachings those days seemed to focus on hypocrisy in religion, on the sorry performance of those claiming to represent his religion, and on the blindness of the people to God in their midst. Remember the "Seven Woes" from Matthew 23?

> "Woe to you, scribes and Pharisees, hypocrites! For you lock people out of the kingdom of heaven . . . Woe to you, scribes and Pharisees, hypocrites! For you cross sea and land to make a single convert, and you make the new convert twice as much a child of hell as yourselves . . . Woe to you, blind guides, who say, 'Whoever swears by the sanctuary is bound by nothing, but whoever swears by the gold of the sanctuary is bound by oath' . . . Woe to you, scribes and Pharisees, hypocrites! For you tithe mint, dill, and cumin, and have neglected the weightier matters of the law: justice and mercy and faith . . . Woe to you, scribes and Pharisees, hypocrites! For you clean the outside of the cup and of the plate, but inside they are full of greed and self-indulgence . . . Woe to you, scribes and Pharisees, hypocrites! For you are like whitewashed tombs, which on the outside look beautiful, but inside they are full of the bones of the dead and of all kinds of filth . . . Woe to you, scribes and Pharisees, hypocrites! For you build the tombs of the prophets and decorate the graves of the righteous, and you say, 'If we had lived in the days of our ancestors, we would not have taken part with them in shedding the blood of the prophets . . . Therefore I send you prophets, sages, and scribes, some of whom you will kill and crucify, and some you will flog in your synagogues and pursue from town to town, so that upon you may come all the righteous blood shed on earth."

That's all a quote, and it is not the kind of preaching calculated to win friends among the powerbrokers of Jerusalem: by the end of the fourth day, Jesus was arrested, and by the end of the fifth he was dead. So much for messianic triumphalism!

Jesus, I should hasten to add, was not ranting against Judaism. He was a Jew himself and was attacking some leaders of his own religion whom he thought were viciously hypocritical. Jesus never attacked anyone else's religion, only those whom he thought corrupted the religion of Israel. We need to take care that our own religious leaders are not hypocrites, that none of them attacks other religions without seeing God in them, that none whitewashes the tomb of American jingoism with the peacemaking words of the gospel, that none supports the pursuit of greed with the good and worthy name of Christian missions, that none speaks well of the corrupt leaders in the corporate world because they contribute heavily to churches, and that none mislead simple people with simplistic theologies. Can we guard against such hypocrisy among ourselves? We have not done well so far.

When Jesus was dragged before Pilate, he did not bluster like an aggrieved rebel. Nor did he posture like a king claiming a throne unjustly denied him by the Roman Empire. He was humble. He said hardly anything. He let the words and actions of his betrayers, accusers, and judge speak for themselves. And they did. For two thousand years the name of Judas is associated with perfidy. The leaders of the temple wanted Jesus dead because they believed he threatened the stability of their relation with the Roman occupation forces, and said it is better that one innocent man die than that the nation be destroyed. Ironically, this promoted, though it did not justify, two thousand years of anti-Semitism, one of the most grievous sins of Christianity. Pontius Pilate is still the epitome of corruption in government, knowing what is just but lacking the courage to carry it out when justice has a price. Even without the resurrection, Jesus the humble teacher won that confrontation on Passion Week. Judas, the temple leaders, and the Romans failed to do the truth. Jesus spoke the truth, and lived the truth. For all he suffered—Jesus's passion means he suffered passively what others did to him—Jesus conquered.

Paul put the point starkly in his great hymn in Philippians. Jesus aboriginally has the form of God. This means, in the conceptions of his age, that he dwelt in the highest heaven with God and had the body and mind appropriate to that heaven. But Jesus then descended to earth and took on the form, not only of a human, but of a human slave. "And being found in human form, he humbled himself and became obedient to the point of death—even death on a cross. Therefore God also highly exalted him and gave him the name that is above every name, so that at the name of Jesus every knee should bend, in heaven and on earth and under the earth, and every tongue should confess that Jesus Christ is Lord, to the glory of God the Father."

Why should we confess that Jesus Christ is Lord? Because he is a political lord, a king? No, he wasn't. Because he beat the Romans? No, he didn't. Because he established the perfect justice of Isaiah's messianic expectation? No, the rabbis were right that things were no better in the next generation. Jesus is Lord because humility of his sort is the stuff of divinity. To speak the truth and accept the consequences is to be humble. To stay with the truth when it costs pain and life itself is to be humble. To be obedient to the point of death—even death on a cross—is to be humble. To hope that one's judgments will win out in the world and yet see no divine intervention to make it so, forsaken on the cross at the point of death, crying, Why? Why? and then saying to the absent Father, "Into your hands I commend my spirit," that is the humility of God.

As we enter into Passion Week, let us have the humble humor to see that our best vehicle is a donkey, not a Humvee. We will not convert the world to democracy by destroying nondemocratic governments and installing our own. That only leads to resistance. We can try humbly to convert the world by speaking the truth about the culture-shaking responsibilities of democracies, and inviting others to those responsibilities. Democracy destroys cultures based on tribal or other community allegiances by insisting on the individualism of one person, one vote; democracy destroys cultures that separate gender roles and class distinctions. Many cultures have much to lose by adopting democracy, and will always lose if it is imposed upon them rather than chosen by them. We need the humility of truth in advertising, even if we ourselves are convinced that democracy is worth the cost. We cannot force a messianic Christian culture on America by saying that God blesses America more than any other nation, by saying that corporate greed is really an expression of freedom, by saying that religious bigotry is upholding standards of humanity, by saying that racial and gender prejudice are justified by the Bible, by saying that exploitation of the environment is proper stewardship, or by saying that neglect of the poor is what they deserve. Yet people have said in recent months that jingoism, corporate greed, bigotry, prejudice, and environmental exploitation are just what the gospel ordered if we can disguise how they are named. We can try humbly to expose and correct those evils by learning and speaking the truth.

You all know that Passion Week is not like opening Christmas presents. Beginning with that cheap and shallow patriotism of the people who threw palms in Jesus's path to his angry attack on the money changers in the temple to his parables and woes about hypocrisy to his betrayal, arrest, and crucifixion, it was a downhill week. By the Sabbath of Holy Saturday, God was off resting, the disciples were hopeless, and Jesus was just dead. There is no guarantee for us that our humble efforts to be peacemakers will succeed, that our invitation to choose democracy will be heeded, that our exposures of hypocrisy in our own religion and culture will go unpunished. The power of evil forces is very great, no less strong now than in Jesus's time. We should expect humility to be crucified. But the more it suffers, the stronger it gets. The more the arrogance of might and hypocrisy strike at the humble, the more their evil is exposed. The humbler we are, like Jesus, the more God is incarnate in our efforts and we are worthy of the glory peculiar to the Lord of Humility. Humility has a power passing the intrigue of Judas, the political compromises of the temple leaders, and the mighty imperial weakness of Pilate. There is power in humility, the power of God. If you want to know what humility is worth, not its power but its worth, come back next week. Amen.

25

Teaching[1]

Isaiah 50:1–91; Philippians 2:1–11; Matthew 21:1–11

Triumph of a cheap and shallow sort on Palm Sunday and triumph of an incomprehensibly glorious sort on Easter Sunday brace intense times of the Christian life. We frequently think about the events of the end of that week: Jesus's last supper with the disciples, the protestations of loyalty and acts of betrayal, the bloody prayer in Gethsemane while the lead disciples doze, the violent arrest, the accusations, trials before the chief priests and Pilate, the scourging and humiliation, the crucifixion and death, the desolation of the Saturday Sabbath, the Easter vigil at the grave, the empty tomb, the resurrection, and the sudden new life of Jesus' friends. The church closely celebrates these end-of-the-week events with liturgies that epitomize their meaning. I invite you to our Tenebre service at 6 here Thursday evening, the service of the Seven Last Words beginning at noon on Friday with the Faurè Requiem, the Easter Vigil Saturday evening at 7 in Robinson Chapel when we shall baptize and receive catechumens, and our Easter sunrise service at 7 and community worship at 11. The Church does well by these end-of-the-week events.

I want to call attention to the beginning of the week, however, where we are now. According to Matthew, Jesus was very edgy, as he had every right to be. If we combine John's account with Matthew's, the events of Holy Week really began several days before. Jesus's teachings had angered some

---

1. Preached March 22, 2005, for the Tuesday Eucharist of Passion Week.

of the elders, scribes, Pharisees, and temple authorities, who had incited a crowd to stone him. Jesus and his disciples escaped and were in hiding when he received word that Lazarus of Bethany, whom he loved, was ill. Jesus waited until Lazarus died so that he could perform a better-than-healing-the-sick miracle, but at great emotional cost to himself. While heading toward Bethany he told his disciples he would be killed. Then the mother of James and John stupidly asked him to make her boys his chief administrators when he established his kingdom: some kingdom! His disciples squabbled about the effrontery of seeking special privilege and he had to scold them. His group passed two blind men who shouted at him and he responded, "What do you want me to do for you?" before he healed them, which they obviously wanted. When he got to Bethany, he broke down and cried twice while meeting with Mary and Martha and raising Lazarus. The night before Palm Sunday they had a party at the home of Lazarus, Mary, and Martha, obviously to celebrate Lazarus's return to the life of the flesh, also to celebrate Jesus, and probably to plan the entry into Jerusalem the next day. That is when Mary poured costly ointment on his feet and wiped them with her hair. Jesus was preoccupied with his coming death, but had to deal with Judas's petty complaint about the cost of the ointment. No wonder the man was on edge.

The crowd hailed him as the kingly Son of David next morning when he entered Jerusalem, sealing his doom with the authorities who saw him as a threat. According to Matthew he went straight to the temple in a rage, overturned the tables of the money changers, and told the authorities that they were making the house of prayer into a den of robbers. People flocked to him in the temple to be healed and he healed them in defiance of the authorities. After going back to Bethany for the night, he returned to the temple on Monday. On the way he passed a fig tree that had no fruit when he was hungry. So he damned it, and it withered at once. Then he used that as an example of the power of faith. This is not the kindly Jesus of Sunday school lore; but it is my friend Jesus, whom I can understand. A man on edge.

Monday through Wednesday Jesus taught in the temple every day. Let me review for you the teachings, one by one, according to Matthew. What do these teachings say to us, this rush of arguments, speeches, and parables? First, Jesus was confronted by the chief priests and elders with a question about the authority by which he worked, and Jesus responded with a trick question that let him refuse to tell about his authority. A man

Teaching

on edge. He told the parable of the man with two sons, one of whom promised to work but did not and the other of whom fussed but did work; Jesus explained that the tax collectors and prostitutes would go to heaven before the hypocritical priests and elders. He told the parable of the landowner who leased a good vineyard to tenants who refused to pay him, killed his messengers, and finally killed his son; Jesus likened the authorities in the temple to the tenants whom God the landowner would put to a miserable death. The power will be taken from the chief priests and Pharisees, he said. He told the parable of the king who gave a wedding banquet for his son, but whose guests declined to come. So the king brought strangers in from the streets, including one man so clueless as not to wear a wedding garment. The man was thrown "into the outer darkness where there will be weeping and gnashing of teeth," because he did not recognize what was real. Jesus was a man on edge. The Pharisees tried to trick Jesus with a question about paying taxes to the Romans, and he answered to render to Caesar the things that are Caesar's and to God the things that are God's, an obvious reference to what he saw as the sorry collaboration between the Jewish leaders and the Roman authorities. The Sadducees then tried to trick him into denying resurrection with the question about whose wife the woman would be in heaven who had successively married seven brothers. Jesus responded by denying sexual differentiation in heaven and then confounded the anti-resurrection theology of the Sadducees by saying that the God of the living, not the dead, was also the God of Abraham, Isaac, and Jacob, who therefore must be still living in some resurrected state. Jesus told the crowds that the scribes and Pharisees who sit on Moses's seat are hypocrites, and he railed at them with seven woes: "Woe to you, scribes and Pharisees, hypocrites," who lock people out of the kingdom of heaven; who make their converts worse than themselves; who teach people false values; who tithe trivial things and neglect the weighty; who look good on the outside but inwardly are full of greedy self-indulgence; who are like whitewashed tombs, full of hypocrisy and lawlessness; who murder the prophets and decorate their graves. Jesus talked about the end times, of the future torture of the disciples, of the coming of God at a time only God knows: stay awake, or a thief will break in. Jesus talked about faithful slaves in the kingdom, about the foolish virgins who were unready for the bridegroom, as the people are unready for God's kingdom, about the slaves who did not invest the talents given them, about the last judgment. Jesus was not gently reminding people of fundamental wisdom, as in the Sermon on the Mount.

He was not preaching peace, love, and already accomplished victory as in the Farewell Discourses in John's account of the Last Supper. He was rushing through to press all his teachings about judgment in the last days into the last days, challenging death to come closer. He was a man on edge.

So should we be on edge, listening to these teachings. For ours is an institution for training chief-priest wannabees, scholar/scribes in waiting, religious reformers like the Pharisees, elders of the church. If we are not on edge, we likely are not resonating with Jesus's own teachings, but are the object lesson of them.

For we live in a time every bit as ungodly as Jesus's time. Our government has led us to attack, conquer, and occupy two countries that did not attack us, for alleged reasons that have proved spurious, at the cost of well over sixty thousand lives: Christian peacemakers should be edgy. Our government pursues economic policies that grow the economy by enriching the rich, impoverishing the poor, reducing entitlements to the needy, outsourcing jobs, borrowing abroad so as to depress the dollar, and mortgaging the future to skyrocketing debt: Christian solidarity with the welfare of the poor should be edgy. Our government deconstructs protections of the environment so as to allow the great corporations to exploit resources we are told are necessary for national security, so as not to have to make friends with nations more than happy to sell us resources: Christian stewards of the Earth should be edgy. Christian criticism of our nation's policies is dangerous these days, even within the Christian community itself. As Jesus the prophet was on edge, so should we be.

Speaking of religion, Second Temple Judaism in Jesus's time was divided into the warring camps of Essenes, Sadducees, Pharisees, and, shortly later, Christians. But that was nothing like the current divisions within Christianity between conservatives and liberals who seem to find no middle ground. Conservatives insist on a conception of Christian life lived under the authority of the Bible with intimate relations between individuals and God and a diminished sense of prophetic justice for society, except in unbiblical matters such as abortion, gay marriage, and a conception of "family values" wholly unknown in biblical times. Liberals insist on a conception of Christian life based on the biblical values of peacemaking, support for the poor and oppressed, respect for God's creation, and inclusive communities tolerant of gender, class, and cultural differences, and yet require an interpretation of the Bible that draws upon current historical and scientific knowledge and is suspicious of any attempt to interpret the

Bible solely on its own terms. How can honest Christians on either side not be on edge about these differences?

The one thing all Christians can have in common is my edgy friend, Jesus. Each of us, in our prayer life, can imagine Jesus as understanding us individually. Although Jesus was not a twenty-first-century person I can imagine him empathizing with me and my troubles and sorrows, my ambitions and fears, my slight accomplishments and my deepest sins that I cannot admit to myself except by imagining Jesus telling me about them. This kind of piety toward Jesus, our friend, is common and central to the Christian life.

Yet we must also reverse the direction of empathy from Jesus to us and imaginatively enter ourselves into Jesus's life, for which we have our gospel texts. The church has led Christians for nearly two millennia to enter into the mind of Christ, which usually means his values and teachings. I urge us to enter into Jesus's life beyond the teachings to his *act* of teaching in those last days, to the situation in which he was ducking arrest to get in a few more days with his disciples, the situation in which he was reconciling himself to his immanent death while dealing with petty concerns of his friends who did not understand, the situation in which he debated his foes whom his teachings about hypocrisy could hardly reconcile, the situation in which he struggled to keep his balance as his mission and life came to an end. He was on edge, and we must understand that. We must be on edge as he was on edge in order to be people "in Christ" in our world, in our religion. We must be on edge as he was in order to enter into his life that is salvation. So I invite you to the table on this Holy Tuesday, not for comfort and consolation this time, nor for satisfaction and nourishment, all of which are among the proper benefits of the Eucharist, but in order to make yours the blood and flesh of our Lord who knew the edgy passion of prophetic teaching in the last hours of the light before the darkness comes. Amen.

26

"Father, into your hands I commend my spirit."[1]

Jesus's final words, at least according to Luke, were, "Father, into your hands I commend my spirit." They are, for us, a model of faithfulness under extreme duress, a kind of faithfulness we would want to have when things go wrong for us, especially when death seems imminent. What a crown it would be for a Christian life to end with these last words! Most of us will probably die unconscious and possibly addled. Some of us will die suddenly without time for thought. But we like to think of our faith as such that these words would express our honest sentiments in extremity.

Scholars have pointed out that these words have a symbolic meaning as well as significance for personal spirituality and reference to the character of Jesus. Jesus returns his spirit or breath—the word *pneuma* means both—to God, who had given him the Holy Spirit at his baptism. God sent Jesus his Holy Spirit to make him who he is. In his dying, because of who he is, he commends his spirit back to God. Then, of course, God gives spirit and breath back again to Jesus at the resurrection. The strength of life comes in giving it away. Part of the meaning of the resurrection is that, if you give your life away, commending your spirit to God, God returns it to you.

---

1. Preached March 26, 2005, Good Friday.

"Father, into your hands I commend my spirit."

The symbolic reference in Jesus's words is not only to his own baptism. When God created Adam, according to Genesis, he first made a clay doll and then breathed his breath into it to give it life. All of us sons and daughters of Adam receive our life-breath from God. In recognition of this, at our death we should return it to its divine source, in this way accepting the life God has given us. Rendering to Caesar the things that are Caesar's and to God the things that are God's, to God belongs our life-spirit. We should remember this when we are not in situations of extremity and think our life is our own, or worse yet someone else's.

Symbolic theology aside, however, contemplate, if you will, the extremity of Jesus's situation. His prophetic mission to recall Israel from hypocrisy and set it on forthright paths of justice and humble worship had failed. He had many followers at first who were enthusiastic when they thought he would change things and then fell away when he did not. He had a few followers who vowed to follow him to the death, but they didn't understand his message, and then they too fell away. The hypocrites he criticized beat him. He was stretched naked on a cross, in front of his mother whom he had spurned, claiming the parentage only of God. Yet his Father God was nowhere to be found. Had he really believed that God would save him and usher in a new kingdom of righteousness? We don't know. But if he did, then his shock must have been an infinite disappointment. Had he really hoped that angels would come and rescue him as Satan's temptation had suggested? If so, he now knew they would not be in time—no winged creatures to pluck him off Mount Doom like Frodo and Samwise for a happy ending. What happened to the God with whom he had been so intimate, whom he encouraged people to call "Abba, Daddy"? Whatever the rich intimacies of his own spiritual life, God did not answer when Jesus prayed bloody sweat at Gethsemane. God was not with him when the temple and Roman authorities decided his fate so unjustly and impersonally. God was not with him when the soldiers whipped, pricked, beat, and humiliated him. Jesus was utterly alone save for the rough hands of the soldiers who were putting him to death as part of a day's work, exposed naked before the impotent eyes of his mother, her women friends, and the disciple he loved. He would hang there unhelped until he died. God was conspicuously absent on Golgotha. Jesus had expected more: "My God, my God, why have you forsaken me!"

This desolate, Jesus's last breath was, "Father, into thy hands I commend my spirit." In saying this, he won the victory. So God turned out to be no intervening help against the bad guys. God turned out to be no inner consoling voice. God turned out to be indifferent to Jesus's mission. God the intimate Father-companion simply wasn't there. God was only the creator of darkness amid cosmic flashes, of seismic earthquakes and natural forces for which human affairs do not register. Jesus then might have hated that indifferent creator. Instead, in dying he commended his spirit to God. He did not lose it to God, he commended it to God.

However you conceive God today, as a transcendent creative act with no personal characteristics or as spiritual person who was just being neglectful, sulking, or treacherous—worse than Judas or Peter—or sadistic in making innocent Jesus suffer for some cosmic purpose, now you conceive God as the object of Jesus's ultimate intentions. In all the desolate horror of that dying, Jesus made God the object of his gratitude for his life-spirit. Though his God, as always imagined before, had vanished, Jesus made him reappear as his life-giving Father, for whom life-taking was part of the gift.

We know so little about God that our conceptions hardly matter. But we do know, because of Jesus's dying words, that we can bind God to ourselves as the object of our ultimate love and gratitude. This does not turn God suddenly into a friendly person. It only makes God the object of those acts *in extremis* by which we become fully persons. We become fully human when we can take as our lover, our beloved, the Creator who gives us this life, so often like a crucifixion, and commend our spirits to that God. Jesus glorified God in his dying, despite God's absence. Jesus glorified himself in his dying, by becoming so human as to thank God for his life and death, and to return his spirit to the one who made his holding it longer untenable. Jesus glorified us in his dying by showing us how to overcome God's indifference, alienation, and distance: if we commend our spirits to God, God is our beloved just as much as we are God's. Amen.

27

Raised with Christ in Newness of Life[1]

Romans 6:1–11; Matthew 28:1–10

As you know, the Jewish day begins with sundown, and so now it is already Easter Day. The Easter Vigil is not waiting for Easter, but a part of Easter waiting for the resurrection to happen or be discovered. We know, of course, what happened and what is going to be celebrated at the resurrection service later on today, in the morning. The liturgical calendar sets our knowing of the Easter events in the mode of memory.

I would like to call attention, however, to the day that has just passed, the Jewish Sabbath, which our calendar calls Holy Saturday. You will recall that the soldiers had to hurry up the crucifixion so that the bodies could be disposed of before Good Friday's sundown, which began the Sabbath, on which no one could work. The Gospels differ over whether Joseph of Arimathea and Nicodemus anointed Jesus's body with spices on Friday afternoon before placing it in the tomb, or the women came to do that Easter morning. But they agree that all observed the Sabbath.

Think what that must have been like. The Sabbath, according to the Genesis passage read earlier, means that God is resting, and surely for the friends of Jesus this must have meant that God was just plain gone. We don't really know what the disciples thought about Jesus prior to the resurrection, because all our Gospels reflect the subsequent theological interpretation of the meaning of Jesus's life. But surely, whatever their religious

1. Preached March 26, 2005, The Easter Vigil.

interpretation, they were personally devastated by his crucifixion. They loved him. Their community was one of love and affection. Just before Palm Sunday they had had a big party for him at the home of Mary, Martha, and Lazarus. His following went far beyond the Twelve, including not only the women commonly mentioned but important people such as Joseph of Arimathea and Nicodemus, and probably many others. Some of them, the leading women and the disciple Jesus loved, had been at the crucifixion and had watched him writhe against the nails until he died. How could they live with that visual memory on Saturday while sitting still for the Sabbath? The other disciples had fled, abandoning Jesus in his mortal pain; some such as Peter had denied him; at least one other, Judas, had betrayed him. How much worse that must have been for them: guilt, compounded by loss, compounded by guilt. If you are not rejoicing over the completion of the glorious creation, which Jesus's friends certainly were not doing, the Sabbath is a dead day. Jesus was dead. God was gone, as good as dead. And the disciples had no life in them.

Sometimes we have times like that. Something happens, someone dies, some duty passes wholly unfulfilled, some project or hope is suddenly cut off utterly, and we are like dead. The strange thing about times like this is the numbness of our response. Serious trauma often brings amnesia. Or at least we have very selective memory, blocking out many of the parts with which we should come to terms. We know we should be grief-stricken, but strangely can't feel anything. We occupy ourselves with distractions: you know how funeral times are preoccupied with cooking food and making arrangements for visiting relatives. I was twelve when my grandmother died, and spent the funeral time, dry-eyed, memorizing the names of the hundred fifty gathered mourners. Truly grieving the trauma of these death-in-life experiences requires time and work. The disciples on Saturday had little time and were forbidden work.

For Jesus's friends, the experiences of his re-appearance came quickly. Doubting Thomas gets special mention in the Gospels because he missed one of the early appearances and said he needed convincing. Nevertheless, the significance of those resurrection appearances could never be appreciated fully until Jesus's friends had come to terms with his devastatingly traumatic death in the first place. The experience could not be just a Friday of death, a Saturday of numb grief, and a Sunday of joy ever after, even though that is the way we epitomize it in our liturgical calendar. No, the meaning of the resurrection for the community of Jesus's friends could only be grasped as they slowly came to terms with the meaning of his death in the first place. Who knows how many years that took?

The Christian recognition of this is expressed in Paul's point that baptism means that we are baptized into the death of Christ Jesus. Baptism in ancient times, and even now in the case of adults, comes at the end of a process of learning what it means to be a Christian. One of the things it means is that we personally reexperience the death of Jesus, come to terms with that in deep existential ways, and accept that death for ourselves.

The beginning way to experience the death of Jesus, of course, is to study Jesus's story in the Gospels. This is always our context for thinking of death. But we also have to understand our own experience as containing death within it, and learn to grieve it. Sometimes this occurs with our experience of the death of people we love, such as grandparents or other relatives. In my case, I simply finessed the existential meaning of my grandmother's death and never did properly recognize or grieve it. When our daughter died, however, there was no escaping death's pain, and I've spent nearly forty years learning to grieve that. I also know grief in the death of my father, brother, and mother, all subsequent to our daughter's death. The literal death of friends and relatives is not the only way by which we come to share in Jesus's death. Traumatic illness and the threat of death for ourselves and those we love might also occasion death's grief. So might traumatic changes in fortune and career, or the dissolution of a marriage. Wars dislocate people. Poverty stamps out hope. Hatred destroys families. In the case of Jesus, he had dreamt of a recovery of righteousness for the people of Israel and the establishment of communities of love of God and neighbor, and he gave his life to that cause. He must have experienced his trial and slow execution as the death of that mission: "My God, my God, why have you forsaken me!" Surely the disciples at first experienced Jesus's death as that mission's failure. Some of us feel strongly about the death of our dreams for our society, and coming to terms with that is a way of experiencing a prophet's death.

For Saint Paul, we experience the trauma of death when we come to recognition of our sins. To be sinners, for him, is to be the walking dead, dead to God and matters of the spirit, live only to the bondage of fleshly exaggeration: greed, selfishness, gluttony, sexual impropriety, and the love of secrets of the night. That sinful state defines who we are, and when we recognize this, we see ourselves to be spiritually dead. Therefore, we need to kill off that self, which we do by sharing in Jesus's death. The death of our sinful selves is very painful, because we love those sins. Becoming a baptized Christian means going with Jesus down into the waters of death where we put to death our sinful souls. This means that we have to know what death means, and grieve it.

Paul's point is that, whereas going down into the waters of death kills the sinful self and lets us know what death truly means, including Jesus's death, rising from the waters of baptism as a new Christian means rising to newness of life.

"For if we have been united with him in a death like his," Paul said,

> we will certainly be united with him in a resurrection like his. We know that our old self was crucified with him so that the body of sin might be destroyed, and we might no longer be enslaved to sin. For whoever has died is freed from sin. But if we have died with Christ, we believe that we will also live with him.

Note that Paul does not say that we will sin no more after baptism. Quite the contrary, much of what he writes in his letters has to do with sin management. Dying with Jesus frees us from bondage to sin, not from the habits of sinning themselves. But the sin that remains in us is like a zombie, a dead body with enough animation still to cause trouble. Sanctification, in its negative moments, is killing off the remaining zombies of sin. In its positive moments, sanctification is building the new life in Christ.

Baptism, in an important but superficial sense, is an initiation rite into the Christian church. Its more profound meaning is that it is a continuing spiritual exercise of dying and rising that lasts a lifetime. The exercise is learning to die by learning what Jesus's death meant, by grieving it so that we know how to grieve our own death, by learning how to enter into Jesus's death so as to die with him and be grieved by Jesus's friends. The spiritual exercise of baptism also means learning how to live in the newness of life that comes out of Jesus's death. This spiritual exercise is never over, for we are always finding new forms of death to undergo and grieve, and new challenges of resurrected life. This is why the controversies over infant baptism are silly: the liturgy of baptism is a momentary event whose deeper reality is never finished in the moment, no matter when the moment happens. The baptized infant has all of life's deaths and renewals to learn, whereas older people might have come through some already. One of the orders of the Christian church is to foster a continuous deepening of the baptism of death and resurrection. Our resurrected life is never more profound than the death from which it arises. This is why some of us are impatient with the spiritual culture of praise music that seeks to get to life without much death.

The Easter Vigil celebrates the newness of life that arises from death. In this borderline moment marking the passage from death to life, let us understand that the depth of life to which we can come is strictly parallel to the depth of death that we have faced. May we be protected from the fatuous joy of an Easter without cost!

The new life in Christ Jesus flashes with astonishing freedom. But the freedom requires first dying to the bondage of sin. Without atonement, our new life is not free. The new life in Christ Jesus sparkles with commitment to bring peace, help the poor, release the oppressed, and bring sight to the blind. But until we have faced the failure of our ethical and political commitments, the commitments of the resurrected life are not strong enough to help us bear their deadly consequences. The new life in Christ gives us the courage and joy that triumphs over death, over the death of our loved ones and even over our own death. But if we have not faced those deaths head-on, tasted the grave's victory and death's sting, then our hope for the new life that triumphs over death will never taste the real victory of the resurrection. Whereas we might hope that salvation consists only in reforming our ways and doing better, the paradoxical Christian gospel is that salvation is as extreme as death on the one hand and resurrection to new life on the other.

Let us think carefully on our hates and lost loves, our pains and sufferings, our frustrations and depressions, our mistakes and failures, our confusions and doubts, our self-delusions and self-hatred, our fragility and impending death: these are not our enemies—they are our friends. For our new life in Christ depends on facing them and grieving the death in them. Newness of life can come only from deaths such as these. Let us taste them. Amen.

28

The Day of Resurrection[1]

Acts 10:31–43; Colossians 3:1–4; John 20:1–18

Hallelujah! Christ is risen. Hallelujah! We are risen. Hallelujah! The nations are risen. Hallelujah! The church is risen. Hallelujah! The world is risen. Hallelujah! More is risen from death and decay than most of you had imagined when you came this morning to celebrate the Easter resurrection of Jesus Christ.

This holiday of resurrection focuses on the resurrection of Jesus of Nazareth, that humble man who spoke the truth about justice and hypocrisy in the wrong places and failed to duck when the political forces of stability and accommodation in Jerusalem lashed out to keep the peace. The week before, Jesus had ridden into Jerusalem, acclaimed by a crowd as a royal descendent of David the Messiah King, a crowd that hoped he would restore Israel's sovereignty and the justice of its internal administration. But Jesus aimed to be no king. He did not gather an army. He addressed no political matters. He claimed no Davidic royalty over against the house of Herod. He aimed to be a teaching Messiah, and his teachings those four days after Palm Sunday exposed the hypocrisy and compromises of the temple leaders and some Pharisees, making him no friends. In the last days he gathered his friends close and pointed out that what he had done was to make them friends with one another, his friends, and God's friends. His Messianic goal was the humble one of creating communities of lovers,

1. Preached March 27, 2005, Easter Day

The Day of Resurrection

whose virtues consisted in making those whom they love better lovers. His love is based on justice, mercy, piety, faith, and hope, and the conviction that love is the actuality of the reconciliation of humankind and God.

Uniting people in reconciling love is a humble task compared with conquering enemies with shock and awe. Yet it is much more difficult. History has seen empire builders by the score, far too many, in fact, and embarrassingly close to home in our time. But the risen Christ's little communities of love have grown and lasted, while every empire has fallen. Each act of Christian kindness is a witness to the humble Christ's resurrection. The exact nature of Jesus's resurrection and his appearances to disciples is inconsistently stated in the Gospels and has been debated ever since. Nevertheless, their effects are evident everywhere that his ongoing love and mercy uplift the poor, free the oppressed, give sight to the blind, and make someone a better lover. Resurrection only makes sense against the presumption of death, and we have seen much death around us. Therefore we shout Hallelujah when we see death reversed in new life.

The author of our text from Colossians points to another resurrection, namely, our own. This may come as a surprise, because at most what we expected for ourselves today is an occasion to wear Easter spring finery. Colossians, however, says that to be baptized in Christ is to die with him to the life of sin and already to be risen with him at the right hand of God. Now if you take literally Christ's heavenly journey with us to the right hand seat next to God, then obviously this is a mistake. We are still only a hundred yards off Commonwealth Avenue. But I think the talk of sitting at God's right hand is a brilliant metaphor, and the reality to which it points is our own state of being free from sin and ready to go with new life because we have accepted the humble man Jesus as our Messiah. Of course, we also live in ordinary life and continue to have the bad habits we had before. Colossians goes on to list fornication, impurity, passion, evil desire, greed, idolatry, anger, wrath, malice, slander, abusive language, and lying. We do these and worse things, but we do not have to: we are not in bondage to them. Colossians says to clean up our act and behave like properly resurrected people. You think you are stuck? Forget it. You have the merciful power of God that raises people to new life coursing through your veins. If you don't have enough, take more! [Gesture to Communion Table] Hallelujah! We are risen.

The nations are risen too. Peter's speech recorded in Acts begins, "I truly understand that God shows no partiality, but in every nation anyone who fears him and does what is right is acceptable to him." He goes on to say that the liberation begun by Jesus in Israel is extended to Rome and then to all the world. What Peter had *in mind* was that people from all nations could be accepted into the Christian church, that membership was not limited to Jews. But what he *said* was more powerful: all are accepted who fear God and do what is right. There are Pagan and Muslim, Hindu and Buddhist, Confucian and Daoist ways of fearing God, each in its own way, and not only Jewish and Christian ways. Justice is commonly defined among religions, even though there are significant cultural variations. God's resurrecting power works in all.

This should be a great relief to us because the nations of the world in our time are a mess, including our own. Jesus's complaints about hypocrisy and injustice among the religious and governmental leaders of his time apply equally well to the nations in the Islamic world, the Marxist world, the world of South Asia, Southeast Asia, East Asia, Africa, Europe, Latin America, and North America. Nevertheless, all these governments can be redeemed. They can be resurrected with less warmongering, less graft, less injustice and prejudice. Hallelujah! We can begin again, even though this requires the slow deconstruction of habits of belligerence, arrogance, greed, inattention to the poor, and oppression.

There's new life for the church too. How in the world can the church be the living body of Christ when it is made up of people such as ourselves who retain so many of the bad habits of the flesh, as Saint Paul delighted to complain? Is the church only an institution? So often the church worries about its institutional self, about increasing its membership, sustaining its continuity, teaching the next generation, competing with alternative institutions, when these concerns seem to be opposite to the obligations of the body of Christ. The body of Christ is to serve the world, teaching justice and mercy, reconciliation and love, and to cultivate the life of love among its members. The church's institutional organizations are only instrumental ways to perform that service, that teaching, that new way of loving life. The resurrection means that we do not have to cling to institutions that are instrumentally dead. The church always has new life and can find new wineskins to culture that life. As a church of the resurrection, we do not have to worry about institutions that are failing in numbers and vigor if we preach the word and serve the world in other ways. As a church of the resurrection, we most definitely do have to worry about institutions that claim the Christian name and yet lack the fruits of the spirit—peacemaking, help

The Day of Resurrection

for the poor, release for the oppressed, stewardship for creation, depth of spirit, courage, joy, and love. Vigorous and growing institutions do exist that, in the name of the Risen Christ, preach war making, inattention to the poor, curtailment of prisoners' rights, exploitation of God's natural creation, fear for the loss of their parochial culture, bitterness about people different from themselves, and hatred of those they deem enemies. The resurrection church leaves that religion of death behind. No Christian need be stuck there. Hallelujah!

Of course, the world of nature is risen today too. Perhaps the most ancient religious rite of humankind is the celebration of the Earth's tilting to meet the sun from which light and life come. Longer days and shorter nights are reasons for joy. Spring means renewal of life: new flowers, new crops, new lambs, and a new baseball season (to speak to the interest of Bostonians). Easter is the Christian's version of the spring festival, of which every religion has some version, tied as it is to the Jewish spring festival of Passover. The power of spring to symbolize new life in every domain goes beyond Christianity and all religions to quicken the hearts of the Scrooges, secularists, and antireligion people. In spring we understand that even the passing of the generations makes way for new generations. In its deepest and broadest meaning, none of us can deny the resurrection of life from death for very long, no matter how we grieve some death or other. The entire world is witness to this resurrection.

The resurrection of Jesus is special to us Christians, however, because we see Jesus to have gone through the worst death: untimely, ruinous of his work, agonizing, humiliating, unjust, undeserved. From this we know that the resurrection message is that our projects' defeat as defined by the world is never the final word, that whatever we suffer for the causes of Christ can be borne, that there is always hope for our community and nation, that the Spirit will always find new ways in the church, that the very violence of cosmic creation from the Big Bang to the Final Dissipation is the eternal receptacle of the transient glories of life, and that even our own frailty, sicknesses, and inevitable death are not as important as the new life we already touch. Let our souls sing with Saint Paul's familiar song: "Who will separate us from the love of Christ? Will hardship, or distress, or persecution, or famine, or nakedness, or peril, or sword? . . .No, in all these things we are more than conquerors through him who loved us. For I am convinced that neither death, nor life, nor angels, nor rulers, nor things present, nor things to come, nor powers, nor height, nor depth, nor anything else in all creation, will be able to separate us from the love of God in Christ Jesus our Lord." Hallelujah! Christ is risen. Amen.

29

Meeting the Risen Christ[1]

Acts 2:14a, 31–41; 1 Peter 1:11–23; Luke 24:11–35

The Scripture readings today and in these several weeks after Easter focus on the formation of the early Christian church out of the fairly large group of Jesus's disciples who had been devastated by his crucifixion and then galvanized to new life as a community by experiences of his resurrection. The reading from Acts is about Peter's sermon at the first Pentecost; we will get to the official celebration of Pentecost in a few weeks. The sermon was addressed to Jews, and it argued that Jesus fulfilled prophecies regarding the Messiah in the Hebrew Bible; our text says that the sermon was extremely successful, calling forth many people to be baptized as Christians. The reading from 1 Peter, a letter ascribed to Peter but probably written about thirty years after his death by someone in Rome to rural Christian congregations in what is now Turkey, aims to define Christian obedience within an alien pagan culture.

From Peter's sermon, probably delivered in the mid-30s of the first century, to the Letter of 1 Peter, probably written in the mid-90s, a vast change had taken place. The community of Jesus's original followers and friends was most likely all Jewish. That community worshiped in the temple with other Jewish groups, and was only one of several groups who claimed to be the continuation of the true Israel in distinction from corrupt forms of Jewish practice. Peter's audience for his sermon included both Jesus's

---

1. Preached April 10, 2005, the third Sunday after Easter.

followers and a large crowd of Jews who had come from all over the Empire to celebrate the Jewish festival of Pentecost, which commemorated the giving of the law, the Torah. Judaism at that time was highly diverse, with not only different parties such as the Sadducees and Pharisees but also Jews from many parts of the world who spoke different languages. We know that among Jesus's followers who formed the Jerusalem Christian church in its earliest years were Jews who spoke Aramaic and those who spoke Greek, the common language of the empire. Philip and Andrew bore Greek names. The first deacons were appointed, including Stephen, whose name in Greek means "crown," to settle disputes between Aramaic-speaking and Greek-speaking widows about who was getting the most benefits from the community purse.

Despite the diversity of language groups within the early Jewish Christian community, or perhaps because of that diversity, the chief theological problem was to define Christianity in relation to the rest of Judaism. The big controversy was whether Gentile converts to Christianity had to become Jews as well, which for the men meant being circumcised and for the women meant cooking kosher. Paul had converted many Gentiles to Christianity and argued that they did not have to become Jews, that Christianity was its own Way, even though for him it was the continuation of the true Israel. Peter slowly came around to Paul's view, and both of them were opposed by James, Jesus's brother, who had become head of the Jerusalem church, outranking both Peter and Paul. You can imagine the church politics involved in that development! Peter sometimes wavered under James's pressure.

The importance of the Gentiles in the early church, and their non-Palestinian context, cannot be underestimated. The earliest writing we have in the New Testament is Paul's first letter to the Thessalonians, probably written in the early 50s, less than twenty years after Peter's Pentecost sermon. That letter is addressed to a congregation of Gentile Christians. All the texts of the New Testament were written in Greek, and the version of the Hebrew Scriptures they used was the Septuagint, a Greek translation.

In the 60s the situation of Jews in the Roman Empire changed radically. In Rome there was a persecution of Jewish groups, including the Christians whom the Romans viewed as Jews. Peter and Paul were martyred in Rome around the year 64. In Palestine the Jews rebelled against the Romans, just as the high priests in Jesus's time had feared. The Roman army swept them away with brutal destruction. You've heard of the heroic last stand of the Jewish rebels on the mountain fortress of Masada where the remaining defenders took their own lives rather than surrender. The temple itself was destroyed in the year 70, two years before Masada.

With the destruction of the temple, the entire priestly apparatus for the practice of the Judaism Jesus and his friends knew, was eliminated. The Sadducees, the priestly party, were gone, and the Pharisees who had adapted to synagogue worship in the Jewish diaspora across the empire became the leading movement toward what we now know as Judaism. James, the head of the Jerusalem church was martyred about the time of Paul and Peter and most of the Christians fled Jerusalem, many to Antioch and beyond. Whereas all the letters of Paul were written while Judaism was oriented to temple worship in Jerusalem, the Gospels and all the other New Testament material were written after everyone knew that kind of Judaism was gone. The problem for Christianity after the destruction of the temple was how to live as a holy people in the midst of a pagan environment, of the sort the Letter of 1 Peter addresses.

We live in a new Rome rather like the old Rome, do we not? Although very much has happened since the end of the first century, and the character of the pagan environment has changed enormously, our own situation remains that of how to live as a holy people in the midst of the hostile environment of new secular imperial economic paganism.

I have gone on so long about the first century of Christian growth because of our gospel text: the story of Jesus appearing to disciples on the road to Emmaus. The man who walked and talked with them did not look like the Jesus they had known so well, and they connected him with Jesus only at the end of the long day when he broke bread. How could they not have recognized his gait or his speech patterns? Even the topic of their conversation, how Jesus fulfilled the prophecy beginning with Moses, was not what Jesus usually had talked about; rather, it was more typical of Peter, as in his Pentecost sermon, or of Stephen's sermon also reported in Acts.

This road to Emmaus incident, this delayed but sudden recognition of a stranger to be Jesus, is a striking disconnect with the rest of the gospel stories about Jesus both before and after Holy Week. These two disciples were not the heroes of the earlier, or even later, stories; only Cleopas was named, and he was never mentioned again. Cleopas and his friend dashed back to the eleven apostles in Jerusalem to tell them about meeting Jesus, when suddenly Jesus appeared in the Jerusalem room, as the continuation of our text this morning says. Then Jesus explained to the other disciples what he had already told the two on the road to Emmaus, as if the two were not there. The talk along the road and the revealing of Jesus in the breaking of bread could have happened anywhere, and it made no difference to the rest of the story of the early church.

It could just as well be set in our time, could it not, with us earnest but historically insignificant Gentile disciples walking down the road in confusion? Someone happens along whom we do not know, and yet after some instruction we recognize Jesus. And because of this, our lives are brought into the resurrection circle.

Like Cleopas and his friend, we live in a time and place where the guardians of religion and government have formed a strange and deadly alliance. Like Caiphas and Pilate conniving to keep the peace even at the price of sacrificing justice, we are told that homeland security requires aggressive attacks on countries that did not attack us, that it requires demonizing the soldiers we attacked and keeping them in prisons without due process, that it requires a drastic exploitation of our environment to make us even more independent of our neighbors than we are, and that it requires a curtailment of liberties at home that were designed in the first place to prevent government and religion from doing evil in our name without our consent. Because the religious forces backing these actions are our religion, and the government our own democratically elected leadership, we are confused in our walk.

In our situation freedom has come to mean the right to consume, economic caring has come to mean enriching the economy for the short-term benefit of the rich, and spiritual discipline has come to mean feeling good about what God has done for us lately. Our culture teaches consumerism whether we believe in it or not. Our tax system is built for increasing the distance between the rich and poor. Our spiritual culture plays to feel-good narcissism on the one hand and irrational fears of threatening neighbors on the other. These are spiritual conditions, not just government policies. No wonder we are confused! The Jesus we thought we knew, who preached peace, justice, mercy, feeding the hungry, clothing the naked, releasing the jailed, enlightening the blind, and who demanded the most astonishing spiritual discipline ever known, has disappeared from public life, entombed in a false gospel. No wonder we are confused!

Yet we have memories of the resurrection. We know that its impact grew from the transforming of Jesus's personal friends to the building of communities of love and discipline all over the world. Our confusion is not as deep as that of Cleopas and his friend, because we are resurrection people. Let us therefore be on the lookout for the resurrected Christ as we walk to Emmaus, or Kenmore Square. Christ will not come to us looking like a Jesus we once knew. Nor will Christ speak or gesture in familiar ways. But someone will come into our lives who can remind us of the message from the Bible about what the Prince of Peace stands for. Someone will recall for us the dignity and goodness of God's creation, and turn us from the disastrous path that is destroying our seas and cities, our forests and fields, for the sake of greed and development. Someone will force us to face the fact that as we treat the poor, the sick, the defenseless, the imprisoned, so we treat the Christ who is all of them. This Christ for us, this person we meet suddenly on the road and recognize in the breaking of bread, might be a different person each week. Surely it will be, for so many such resurrection appearances happen all around us, and we do know how to recognize them.

My friends, the point is deeper, because we ourselves are commissioned to be for the people what Jesus was to his disciples. I'm sorry to tell you that this means we need to be the resurrected Christ for one another and for the rest of the world. You might not think you are up to it. But you are. We know the Bible. We know its prophetic critique of societies such as our own. We know how to recognize the demands of spiritual discipline. We know how to tell the difference between loving enemies and demonizing them as "insurgents" against our will. We know how human economic expectations need to be scaled back to what God's creation can support with equal opportunity for all people and without the disasters of global warming. We know how the ignorant and unskilled need education. We know how the poor need help. We know how the sick need healing, how the oppressed need justice, how the grieving need comfort. We know how the spiritual life needs exercise, with daily prayer, meditation, study, and the companionship of kindred, seeking souls. We know the joy of a life that puts down death, that knows dignity in humility, that sings God's song in the arts, that finds God's mind in science, that touches God's power in the heaving of oceans, that trembles before God's beauty in sunsets, that feels God's depths in the starry night sky, and that embraces the light of God's dawn like a bridegroom emerging from his pavilion. Being people of the resurrection, graced with this knowledge, it is our calling to talk to people on the road and surprise them with the living Christ. Amen.

30

To Follow the Shepherd[1]

Acts 2:41–47; 1 Peter 2:19–25; John 10:1–10

Our three texts today are embarrassing, each in its own way. The passage from Acts presents the most idealized image of the early church that you can imagine. A community of over three thousand people devoting themselves to learning from the apostles, fellowship, common Eucharistic meals, prayer, miracles, pious awe, sharing everything in common, spending much time in the temple, enjoying one another with glad and generous hearts, praising God, and gaining the respect of the people, with the result that the community continued to grow every day. Who of you who has spent any time in church at all would believe this unalloyed evangelistic success? This is an odd passage even for the Bible. It follows immediately upon a passage in which Peter berates sinners to save themselves by accepting Jesus as the Messiah, and it is followed by a long story in which Peter and John get thrown into jail for healing and teaching in the temple, texts which are much more typical biblical narratives. Then the next thing that happens is that two new converts try to cheat the rule of owning everything in common by keeping some of the proceeds of their property and they are struck dead. The ideal community does not last long. In fact, our idealized text is embarrassingly like a Hallmark Card version of church history.

The text from 1 Peter is embarrassing in two ways. The first is that the lectionary editors start the passage with the second sentence of the

1. Preached April 17, 2005, the fourth Sunday after Easter.

paragraph. The first sentence reads: "Slaves, accept the authority of your masters with all deference, not only those who are kind and gentle but also those who are harsh." The call to endure suffering really refers to the suffering of slavery, which our editors try to hide from us. While this text is not exactly an endorsement of slavery, it certainly is a refusal to criticize it even when the slavery is torture. The second way this passage is embarrassing is that it seems to say that suffering itself is good, and that because Jesus suffered, we also should suffer. This text has been cited to justify abuse of women who are supposed to feel good about the suffering they bear. The sentence immediately following our passage says: "Wives, in the same way, accept the authority of your husbands, so that, even if some of them do not obey the word, they may be won over without a word by their wives' conduct, when they see the purity and reverence of your lives." The image of brutal men being tamed by the docile suffering of their brutalized women is a deep embarrassment. Like slavery, the debased status of women was part of the general Roman society of the time, and we have rejected both on Christian grounds.

The gospel text from John is embarrassing because it likens us to sheep. Sheep are very stupid. They keep their nose down and wander from the path. Sheep need shepherds or they get lost. We surely are not so stupid and dependent, are we? To suggest that Jesus is a shepherd is strange imagery too. Except for the story of shepherds coming to praise his birth, he never dealt with them. Jesus was a town boy whose family was in the building trades. His friends were fishermen, and the activities of his childhood and youth were shaped by the fact that the Romans were building a new city close to his hometown. The local economy was devoted to supplying that construction effort. Jesus was far from the pastoral life that dominated the imagery of the older Hebrew Bible. I suggest we just get over the embarrassingly unflattering suggestion that we are sheep and Jesus is a shepherd and ask what the text is about.

The text is about abundant life, of course. Jesus says he is the way to abundant life, and uses two images for this. To reach abundant life is like going through a gate. Jesus likens himself both to the gate itself, and to the gatekeeper. What is striking about our text, however, is the repeated juxtaposition of Jesus as the proper leader to the thieves and bandits, that is, the false leaders who will take the lambs to slaughter. Jesus, the true shepherd, will lay down his life for the sheep, a reference to the crucifixion; but the hired-hand shepherd will flee when the wolf or thief comes. Or the butcher.

Who did Jesus have in mind as the thieves and bandits? Our passage comes right after Jesus's encounter with the Pharisees who refused to believe that Jesus had healed the blind man, and who badgered both the man and his parents to renounce Jesus. Those were the bandits he was referring to, people in his own religion, the Judaism of his time, who were dishonest, sneaky, and manipulative. Those Pharisees, remember, threatened the formerly blind man's parents with excommunication from the temple if they testified to Jesus, so they kept quiet; their son did not keep quiet, and the Pharisees did throw him out of the temple. That was hypocrisy. The objects of Jesus's attack in our passage were the corrupters of religion.

Abundant life, therefore, means true and honest religion, which Jesus defined as doing the work of God the Father. What is that work? Doing what Jesus did when he claimed that he, like everyone to whom the word of God comes, is a son of God. Read the rest of John chapter 10 for this argument. So what was it that Jesus did? What was his work, which he claimed was divine work? The Gospel of John makes it very clear that Jesus's work was to create communities of love that have a double effect. One effect of loving communities is to overcome the alienation among people that manifests itself in hatred and injustice. The other is to overcome the alienation between God and people that manifests itself in our sinful rejection of God and God's work. This is to say, Jesus's work was to bring about communities of love of neighbor and love of God. The consequence of Jesus's work is redemption. Its content is life abundant. Jesus's work is the gateway to redemption and life abundant, which he often called eternal life.

Jesus brought four things to his work. One was his positive preaching about how to live as friends and lovers together. Regarding our human communities he preached justice and mercy, care and forgiveness, peacemaking and humility, all as conditions for love. Regarding our friendship with God, Jesus preached prayer, study of the Scriptures, and mutual help through traditional means of grace for the attainment of intimacy with God. We all know these familiar positive points of Jesus's teaching. Can we not take these as virtues for our own lives?

The second component of Jesus's work was his skilled denunciation of hypocrisy. Again and again Jesus exposed the corruption of the institutions and teachings of his own religion by hypocritical leaders. He attacked the selfishness that led to the exploitation of the poor and powerless, a selfishness that decorated itself in the trappings of righteousness. This denunciation of hypocrisy was one of the principal offenses that got him in trouble with the authorities. Is it not incumbent on us, too, to name hypocrisy when we see it, particularly in our religion?

The third component of Jesus's work was actually helping people, usually by healing the sick and demented. He took sickness and sin to be symptoms of a broken world that needs redemption. The healing of these is itself a sign of God's work to complete and redeem creation. We too can be healers of sickness and restorers of sinners to grace, can we not?

The fourth and most important component in Jesus's work was his own loving and winsome person. People who met Jesus loved him. Not everyone, of course, not those caught in the bonds of hypocrisy. But sinners loved him because of his own manifest love for them. Rich people loved him, poor people loved him, flagrant sinners loved him, and the very righteous, whose only flaw was an inability to release their possessions, loved him. He worked so hard with his disciples, teaching and reproving them, but always loving them; and they loved him in return. Read the fourteenth through seventeenth chapters of John to see how Jesus's love brought his disciples to be a community of love and friendship with one another and with God. Jesus's disciples know the voice of their Lord, as the sheep know the voice of their own shepherd, because they love that voice, and love the love in that voice.

Our own spiritual lives are good if we fervently pursue justice and mercy, care and forgiveness, peacemaking and humility, all these virtues that make for positive, loving communities. Our spiritual lives are better if, in addition, we go through the purifying fires of rooting out hypocrisy. Hypocrisy in our institutions, our leaders, and friends, is dangerous to reveal. Hypocrisy in ourselves is painful to reveal. Yet we cannot face God without the honesty to admit who we are, save by the welcoming mercy of God that overlooks our self-deceptions and simultaneously shines light upon them. Jesus taught that our temptations to hypocrisy are Satanically inspired. In matters of honesty, our spiritual lives include a war against the Enemy.

Our spiritual lives are even better if, in addition to the positive virtues of love and the ruthless unmasking of hypocrisy, we actually do something to help people. Jesus taught that service to others is essential to spiritual life. The virtues proper to a loving community are hollow, in fact hypocritical, if they are not practically expressed in feeding the hungry, clothing the naked, visiting the prisoners, making peace, deconstructing the structures of oppression, and building a more just world. Devoting our lives in service to others in the name of God is essential to our spiritual lives.

Our spiritual lives are filled to abundance, however, if in addition to all these we are in love with Jesus. Christians find eternal life most abundantly in loving Jesus. Although we are at some distance from Jesus compared with his immediate disciples, we can hear his voice in the Bible. We can feel his love in our contemporaries who are filled with the love of Jesus. We can cultivate our imagination in meditation and prayer to understanding how Jesus could love us personally. We are each unique, with our own situations and personal relations, our own stations and ambitions, our own foibles and sins, our own gifts and dark secrets. To understand the love of Jesus for us personally, we need to imagine him addressing each part of us, companioning us in our peak experiences, bearing us up in our deepest sins and failures, working with us day by day. This imaginative life of sharing love with Jesus is the heart of Christian spiritual life. All our virtues, our truth-speaking, and our good works feed into this spiritual imagination of divine friendship. The power of that spiritual imagination opens us to God. For, the love we find for ourselves in Jesus our friend is the love God has for us. As we reciprocate that love in our love of Jesus, we learn to love the Creator who gives us this world.

Now we can understand the passage in 1 Peter about suffering. Our world is full of suffering, and that is among the gifts of God: not all gifts are happy ones. But by enduring the sufferings of life we learn to think with Jesus how he loves us and how we love him, and thus we learn better how to love God. And as for that embarrassing idealized view of the church that could not last, it serves as an ideal by which we test the fruits of Christian love. We measure the depth of our understanding of Jesus's teachings, our grasp of his critique of hypocrisy, our commitment to his work, and our mutual devotion and friendship, when we see the effects of our spiritual life tending toward that ideal. That ideal sketches the fruits by which increasing abundance of life is measured.

Though we balk to think of ourselves as sheep, we do know the gate to abundant life. We know Jesus, the gatekeeper, and can respond to his call. Although the shepherd takes us over demanding paths of virtue, confession of hypocrisy, and works, it is his winsomeness that attracts and leads us. What I have called the knowledge and love of God in imagination is what the tradition has called the work of the Holy Spirit. Jesus the Christ, the Good Shepherd, is alive with us in God's Spirit. It is our privilege, and great happiness, to follow him. Amen.

31

"I Am the Way, the Truth, and the Life"[1]

Acts 7:51–60; 1 Peter 2:1–10; John 14:1–14

I am grateful to the Reverend Doctor Gomes for the invitation to preach here today, a great honor. He is to be congratulated and envied for his sabbatical, and I sincerely hope that he is enjoying a term of refreshment in which he can look with pleasure on his accomplishments and prepare himself for the work ahead. After all, the sabbatical is the only part of the academic enterprise invented directly by God, as recounted in the Genesis discussion of creation regarding the seventh day.

Our gospel contains the famous, or notorious, saying by Jesus: "I am the Way, the Truth, and the Life. No one comes to the Father except through me." The notoriety comes from its negative part: "no one comes to the Father except through me." This sometimes has been taken to be a rejection of religions other than Christianity. Yet there is no evidence that Jesus had that in mind at all. In every instance, save one, of Jesus's recorded encounters with people who were not Jews like himself, he was positively impressed with their faith and helped them just as he did his own kind. Think of his dealings with the Samaritan woman at the well, the Canaanite woman who ate the crumbs under his table, or the Roman centurion whose

---

1. Preached in Memorial Church, Harvard University, Cambridge, Massachusetts, on April 24, 2005, for the fifth Sunday after Easter, at the invitation of the Rev. Dr. Peter Gomes, Chaplain of Harvard University.

boy he healed. The exception was Jesus's encounter with Pontius Pilate, and there the issue was not religious affiliation but honest government.

The positive part of Jesus's saying is at the center of defining the Christian Way. Those of us who are Christians take this saying as our inmost identification: Jesus is our way, truth, and life. At the same time it is a Way that can be followed by anyone who is willing to do the work Jesus did. In Jesus's culture and time, a son often was defined as inheriting his father's estate and work. So, we infer that Jesus was trained as a carpenter because Joseph was. More importantly, Jesus defined himself as Son of God for the reason that he did God his Father's work, as he said in our text. Luke's genealogy of Jesus runs back through the generations and ends, "son of Cainan, son of Enos, son of Seth, son of Adam, son of God." I'm sorry that the ancient sensibilities left women out of this order of things; yet it takes only a little modern imagination to see that daughters too can be identified through the work of the parent, even the divine parent.

Whatever other meanings might belong to the phrase "Son of God" as applied to Jesus in the New Testament, Jesus says in our text that he is Son of God because he does God's work. Because of the unity of that Father-Son work, he can return to God. Moreover, because he had taught the disciples also to do God's work, they too can return to God. This is the plot behind the discussion of Jesus returning to the Father and preparing a place for the disciples. He says that they already know the way to the Father. Flustered, Thomas says they do not know the way. Frustrated, Jesus says "I am the way," etc., and you have been with me long enough to know me. He says that, if the disciples do not believe in him as such, at least they can believe in the work that he did among them. I take this to mean that non-Christian people can still be in unity with Jesus and God by doing his work.

We know from the text immediately following ours, which is in the lectionary for next Sunday, that his work has been to build communities of love, with all this entails regarding justice, peacemaking, forgiveness and mercy, clothing the naked, feeding the hungry, opening the eyes of the blind, visiting those in prison, showing hospitality to those different from ourselves, embracing our enemies, and enduring with patience all the high costs that go with loving communities. We each of us know close analogues to these works in our own situation. Many things in our country need to be changed if we are to uphold straight justice for rich corporate crooks as well as petty thieves from the ghetto; if we are to make peace rather than war to get our way; if we are to practice forgiveness and mercy rather

"I Am the Way, the Truth, and the Life"

than vengeance against those who lash out against us; if we are to care for the poor rather than reduce entitlements to pay for tax cuts; if we are to educate those most in need in addition to those who already come from a culture of learning; if we are to release political prisoners and those who defended their country against us when we attacked; if we are to offer God's hospitality to all creatures instead of only those who look, think, and act like us; if we insist that no one can be regarded as an enemy without also being the object of our love; and if we are willing to endure the constant defeats in small as well as large things as we strive to live out loving communities in our families, friendships, neighborhoods, civic units, nation, and world. This is the old story of the work of the Christian Way: you know it, and we have a ways to go. Yet nothing in what I just listed as the works of a Christian, deriving from Jesus's work, and in unity with God's work in creation and redemption, requires that one be self-identified with Jesus or Christianity. Anyone can take on that work, which we, if not they, know is in continuity with God and Christ's work.

Permit me to focus in more detail, however, on the meaning for Christians of "the way, the truth, and the life." The "Christian Way," I think, has two main forms. The first form is what I call the "church Christian Way," which most people identify with Christianity. However you define the church—and I advise you to duck when professional theologians start arguing about that—it includes a vast array of institutional forms that preserve the memory of Jesus and his work, and that interpret how that work extends from his Galilean context through all the cultures of the world reached by Christians. The church has a rich literature and hymnody, many forms of assembly, a calendar for rehearsing epitomes of the Christian life, and many social communities in which people live the particulars of their lives from birth to work to death.

The second form of the Christian Way, by contrast, is a "cultural Way" and consists in struggling to understand our secular situation in Christian terms, to discover what Christian terms mean in our situation, and to learn how to be faithful to Jesus's work in secular life. People in this second way might also belong to a Christian congregation and identify with the church, but that is not their center of gravity as it is for people who are on the church way. This second, cultural Christian Way, relativizes the church as one institution among many, and activates faith outside it. One thinks of poets such as T. S. Eliot, Robert Frost, and Geoffrey Hill, whose work has been the leading edge of Christian thinking, but who have not been thinking only in and for the church. The theologian Paul Tillich was a bit like this, thinking for the world rather than the church, and he is held in suspicion by many church theologians for that fact. I suspect that in a university such as this, though not of course in Memorial Church this morning, many people work predominantly on the cultural Christian Way rather than the church Christian Way.

Jesus is the Way and the Truth. To speak of Jesus being the Truth supposes something like the following. Merely to fall into a category to find an identity is one thing. To fulfill that categorical identity by being an exemplary or fully realized member of the category is quite another. For instance, many coloratura sopranos have sung, but Lily Pons and Joan Sutherland were true coloraturas. Many baseball players have played, but Babe Ruth, Stan Musial, and Ted Williams were true players. There are many Christians like ourselves who identify with taking on Christ and his work, and yet most of us are schlubs. The true Christians are the saints.

That Jesus is the truth for Christians means that Christians are in transition to become more like him, more Christ-like, more fully integrated into God's work in the world, more effective in it, more emptied out into it. This transformation deepens and ramifies the symbols of Christian piety. Consider the Lord's Prayer by reflecting on the creation by virtue of which God is called Father, and see it to encompass a universe of vast age and extent, violent beyond imagination, indifferent to human needs save in the fragile environment of the third planet out from Sol on the edge of a minor galaxy. Our life-world is an engine of consumption, micro-organisms eating smaller ones and in turn being eaten by larger ones. Species live on other species and are prey in turn, finally vanishing to extinction when their habitat no longer tolerates them. The blood of human beings has about the same saline proportion as the seas from which our slime-mold ancestors emerged, and we bear the genes of fish, frogs, snakes, and tigers, as well as the sensitivities of the founders of human civilization. So when we pray the Lord's Prayer in transition to greater spiritual depth, the meaning of "Our Father who art in heaven" is that God is the Father of all that, a wild, fierce, and destroying Father as well as the Father of justice and human order. Moreover *we* are part of all that creatureliness down to the saltiness of our blood, the snake in our genes, and the lives of others in our diet. The truth of Christ is not the tame stuff we tell our kids. The truth of Christ is the awesome, wild, and often unbalanced character that is able to stand in the divine winds of cosmic blasts, to stare down the abyss of suffering and

"I Am the Way, the Truth, and the Life"

fiery glory only poets can imagine, to love the God who leaves us nailed to crosses, to take up the work of our Beloved whose precious loving communities heave atop the tectonic plates of brute force, passion, blood, and poetry. Did you ever wonder why the central ritual of Christianity is a cannibal rite in which we symbolically eat the flesh and drink the blood of our Founder? It is because nothing any tamer could present the awesome depth of the Truth of Christ into which we would be transformed.

Jesus is the Way, the Truth, and the Life. That Jesus is "the Life" pulls together many different senses in which the image of life is used in Christian Scripture. In Genesis God breathed into the clay doll and Adam became a living being. In Deuteronomy God set the choice between life and death and urged the people to choose the life of obedience that would lead to prosperity and flourishing of Israel. In Ezekiel God reknit the dead, dry bones and breathed life into the people of Israel so that they would again be united and flourish. Jesus repeatedly brought the dead back to life, although they were not necessarily better off spiritually than before they had sickened and died. On the other hand, people might be physically alive and yet spiritually dead, when the Holy Spirit summons them to new spiritual life in Christ. Jesus's resurrection from physical death introduced a new level of spiritual life as fellowship with God, characterized by the symbol of the ascension, and yet Jesus claimed already to have had that fellowship in his last supper with the disciples prior to his death, and said that with the Holy Spirit they too could have that fellowship of resurrection to life with God within this life. To follow Jesus's Way in our work, to press on toward him as the wild Truth of our lives, is to inhabit a life that combines and intensifies all these senses of Jesus as the Life.

Jesus's term for this in John's Gospel is "eternal life." Eternal life embraces the future but is a quality of present life. Eternal life incorporates the past, adding life to the inanimate, overcoming death in present abundant life. Yet the abundance of eternal life is not like worldly prosperity—often quite the contrary: its signature, after all, is the cross. Jesus's Way and Truth lead to participation in the eternal abundance of God's life. Jesus said, "the Father and I are one." We can imagine only the tiniest slice of the eternal abundance of divine life, but even this little includes the winds of cosmic blasts and the abyss of suffering and fiery glory. It includes also within our ken the fierce fecundity of God's creative love that throws up countless galaxies, swarms of species, and rivers of power for healing and new chances. While on Jesus's Way and living in his Truth, we reflect back this divine, cosmic love and then receive again our love returned and magnified, ever more creative, then share it out with others, receive it back, and send it yet again in new directions. God's eternal abundance is a living engine of creative love in which we share through every pulse of loving God and neighbor. We love and are loved more than we know. By taking Jesus as the Way, the Truth, and the Life, we know the way into the divine Father, just as Jesus said in our text. With love's powers we bear up under all trials and enter ever more deeply into the wild abundance of divine immensity. This Way, Truth, and Life are open to all. But thanks be to God for our Rabbi Jesus Christ, who shows us the Way, the Truth, and the Life. Amen.

32

Forms of Love[1]

Acts 17:21–31; 1 Peter 3:11–22; John 14:11–21

Our gospel text today lies in the middle of a long passage running from chapter 13 to chapter 17 in which John the Evangelist recounts Jesus's conversation with his disciples at the Last Supper, beginning with Jesus washing the disciples' feet. Scholars call this the Farewell Discourse, and it is far longer than any other conversation recorded by John or the other Gospel writers. John's text was written about sixty years after the events it records, and of course we have no way of knowing how accurate it is to the actual conversation. Matthew, Mark, and Luke say almost nothing about that last conversation except remarks having to do with the blessing of the bread and wine from which we take our eucharistic ritual, something John omits to mention. John's intent was to give a kind of theological summary of Jesus's sense of his mission and directions for the disciples. So he selected sayings of Jesus, or perhaps his own paraphrases, that add up to this theological statement as understood by John and his community. Whether Jesus actually said these things in this order on this occasion is not the point, although in many other respects John is the most historically accurate of the Gospels. The Farewell Discourse is edited with John's understanding of Jesus's theology, the most comprehensive understanding we have in the New Testament. This discourse is the Jesus we know through the earliest witnesses.

1. Preached May 1, 2005, the sixth Sunday after Easter.

Our text for today is the part of the Farewell Discourse in which Jesus says that, if the disciples love him, they will keep his commandments. Notice that the motivation for keeping the commandments is that the disciples love Jesus, as he has loved them and taught them to love one another. All this comes, Jesus says, because God the Father loves him and them, and Jesus's work has been to demonstrate this love. Under ordinary circumstances, we might think that the proper motivation for keeping the commandments is simply that they are obligatory. Or if we are selfish, we might think that the motivation is to get some divinely bestowed reward or avoid punishment. For Jesus, however, the fundamental phenomenon of the faith, the most important religious reality, is love. His disciples, whom we now call Christians, are supposed to take this love as the grounding context for all Christian life. When they, or we, do this, Jesus says that we have the Holy Spirit as an advocate and guide for how to live in a world full of troubles.

Our text comes shortly after this remarkable saying by Jesus: "I give you a new commandment, that you love one another. Just as I have loved you, you also should love one another. By this everyone will know that you are my disciples, if you have love for one another." Most of the Farewell Discourse has to do with explicating this commandment, which serves as a kind of summary for all the other commandments of Jesus concerning justice, mercy, help for the poor, release of prisoners, opening the eyes of the blind, and the rest. Jesus was particularly concerned about the avoidance of hypocrisy and in our text calls the Holy Spirit the Spirit of Truth. We know the general content of Jesus's teachings, which he summed up elsewhere as loving God with all our heart, mind, soul, and strength, and our neighbor as our self. In John's Gospel, our capacity to love one another is intimately bound up with God's love for us and our love for God, as understood through Jesus and what he did.

Now, the problem with this spirituality of love is that it can become syrupy piety that makes us feel good while disguising the fact that we live in anything but loving ways. So reflect with me, if you will, on what forms love might take in our lives so that it might be the genuine center of the Christian life. I want to consider four forms of love: social love, cultural love, family love, and love among friends.

Social love might be hard to think of as love, because society is where institutions put us in touch with people we do not know personally. Of the themes of Jesus's teachings, justice and peacemaking are the most prominent elements of social love. Justice has three classic forms. Distributive justice is the fair distribution of the world's goods and opportunities. What fairness consists in might be debatable in some situations, but injustice in distribution is cheating and the abuse of power, about which Jesus was scathing. Our own nation's current policies get poor marks for distributive justice, withdrawing entitlements for the poor to pay for tax cuts for the rich and their wars to secure economic dominance; we also do not do well in protecting the resources of the environment. Retributive justice is the determination of guilt regarding evildoers, holding them responsible, and exacting punishment appropriate to the crime. Jesus had a prophet's anger regarding evildoers, particularly those with social power. But paradoxically he also hailed mercy and forgiveness as the proper responses to guilt, urging the wicked to repent and amend their ways. Our justice system seems to favor those who can afford fancy lawyers and crushes the souls of the poor, for whom prison seems a part of their culture. Restorative justice, the third kind, aims to reconcile aggrieved parties who have been hurt by injustice and who might continue on a downward spiral of recrimination if mutual respect is not restored. Restorative justice became popular first in South Africa where its institutions allowed the victims of apartheid to confront their oppressors and forced the oppressors to sit and listen. Restorative justice, about which we have courses here in the Boston University School of Theology, aims to heal social wounds, and is perhaps the clearest form of social love. Peacemaking, of course, is the center of Christian activism at the social level and sets Christians in our time against our government's policy of the use of force to get our way. War is never kind, to the winners or losers, even when it is necessary.

Cultural love is closely tied to social love, and it has to do with those institutions and practices that give meaning to our lives. Our souls are formed around patterns of ethnic, linguistic, culinary, historical, and mythic identity. We have wealthy cultures and modest cultures, youth cultures and mature cultures; pity the cities that do not have the Red Sox. Our souls find meaning and fulfillment in the particularities of culture. Within contemporary Christianity, some people find meaning in high-church liturgies, others in free-church worship, some in classical sacred music, others in the culture of praise music. Cultures are always particular and have certain patterns that exclude other patterns. Yet the principal Christian model of love in all this is to celebrate inclusive table fellowship. Jesus ate with rich and poor, Jew and Gentile, saint and sinner. His example of the good neighbor was a Samaritan whose culture was in a hostile relation to

Jesus's own. In our time the great issues of inclusiveness have to do with racism, equality for women, full acceptance of gay and lesbian people, and overcoming national chauvinism in the clash of civilizations. A large group in America has defined the particularity of its cultural identity in terms of white superiority, keeping women in unfree roles, misrepresenting gay and lesbian people as intrinsically sinful, and caricaturing other cultures. The attempt to force this narrow cultural identity on others is an exercise in cultural hate. Cultural love seeks ways to respect the particularity of cultures while insisting that respectable cultures respect others.

Family love is the most familiar form of love in our society, though it was not always so. In Jesus's time families were difficult economic institutions, placing heavy burdens on women and those with no families. For us, however, marriages are supposed to be founded on love, and are the social institutions in which children learn how to love, parents learn to love children, siblings learn to love those with whom they compete, and nuclear families learn to love those others who are outside their circle. To be sure, contemporary families can be corrupted to replace genuine love with consumerist selections and rejections of mates, to put women into new forms of bondage, to make life hell for gay and lesbian children, and to teach distortion and fear of people different from oneself. How ironic that many people who oppose gay marriage do so in the name of family values, when marriage is the very thing we should offer gay and lesbian people if it is so much the institution valuing love! What kind of family values do they have in mind? Certainly not love. The forms of family love foster the flourishing of all those in the family and those outside who are affected by the family.

Doubts about the family, at least as it was structured in his time, are probably what led Jesus to say nothing good about it and explicitly to substitute his voluntary organization of friends as the primary vehicle for his commandment to love one another. His relationship with the disciples has become the model for the church in a certain respect. Of course the church is large enough to be a society, and particular enough to be a culture. Sometimes the church identifies with families so much that those without families are left out. Jesus's point, however, is that a true community of loving friends breaks through the limitations of all family, cultural, and social structures. Where social love breaks down with injustice and warmongering, the community of Jesus's friends needs to be a counterforce. Where cultural love breaks down with exclusion and bigotry, the community of Jesus's friends needs to create an inclusive pattern of meaning. When family love breaks down into bondage and chauvinism, Jesus's friends need to set people free and embrace those who otherwise have no place.

Jesus called his friends together for a mission, actually a continuation of his own mission, which is to create communities of friends who love one another. To love other people is not just to have a sentiment about them, but to make them better people, which means, to make them better lovers. Love is false unless it includes justice, deference to those different from ourselves, commitment to engage the issues of our time, and taking responsibility for what we make of ourselves. To make someone a better lover requires helping them with all these things, at the social, cultural, and familial levels. This commandment to love is very daunting, is it not? Are we not then blessed to have Jesus's example of friendship? The love in friendship is where our souls are brought into existence. The greatest hurt to our souls comes from failed friendship. The greatest power of healing is in merciful, loving friendship. Our friends are with us in the peak moments of experience, and also in the depths of despair; they companion us daily. They forgive us our forgetfulness and encourage us to push always to better life. The greatest friend was Jesus, whose love of the unruly disciples brought them to love one another, and whose acceptance of God's love allowed him, and the disciples, to love God in return. Is that not the reconciliation of ourselves to God and one another? Praise be to God for Jesus our Friend who redeems our life and whose Spirit can make Jesus our Beloved. Amen.

33

Freedom of the Spirit[1]

Acts 2:1–21; 1 Corinthians 12:3b–13; John 7:31–39

Pentecost Sunday celebrates the occasion described in our reading from Acts when the Holy Spirit came upon Jesus's disciples as they were gathered together shortly after his death and ascension. The Greek word for "Spirit" also means "wind" and "breath" and, according to Acts, the Spirit came with the sound of a mighty wind, with tongues of fire resting on the heads of the disciples. A tongue of fire, like wind symbolizing the Holy Spirit, is the official symbol of the United Methodist Church. Pentecost itself was a Jewish holiday celebrating the giving of the law, the Torah, to Moses. The disciples were in Jerusalem, which was filled with Jewish pilgrims for the festival of Pentecost from all over the Roman Empire. Being filled with the Spirit, the disciples were able to speak to each group of pilgrims in the language of their homelands. Our text lists the languages and homelands.

Scholars have pointed out that this speaking in many languages was very different from the glossalalia or "speaking in tongues," using nonsense words, which later characterized some Christian communities, for instance, Paul's congregation in Corinth. Rather, the Pentecost language phenomenon was intelligible communication.

In our gospel text from John, Jesus predicts that the Holy Spirit would come to his believers after he had been glorified, that is, after he had been killed, raised, and drawn into heaven. Jesus likens the Spirit to rivers of

1. Preached May 15, 2005, Pentecost Sunday.

Freedom of the Spirit

living waters, not fire or wind this time. He called himself the water of life. The general context for this speech of Jesus was the Jewish festival of Booths that commemorates the Exodus wandering in the wilderness, and the specific context, the last day of the festival, remembers the occasion when God provided water from a rock to save the parched Israelites: hence Jesus's image of the water of life. This festival also celebrates the anticipation of the Messiah to save the people. Peter's sermon, quoted in our text from Acts, cites the prophet Joel's proclamation that the Holy Spirit would be poured out "upon all flesh, and your sons and your daughters shall prophesy, and your young men shall see visions, and your old men shall dream dreams." This would happen on the "day of the Lord," that is, when the Messiah comes.

In the New Testament and in the Christian interpretation of the Hebrew Scriptures, the Holy Spirit is closely associated with Jesus as the Messiah. In John's Gospel, Jesus says the Spirit will come to the disciples after he is gone to guide and sustain them, to interpret to them the meaning of his life and the direction of theirs. Christianity is a Trinitarian religion because it believes that, just as Jesus is God in some sense, so is the Holy Spirit. We baptize and bless others and ourselves in the name of the Father, the Son, and the Holy Spirit.

And yet! And yet, the Holy Spirit has never been received comfortably within the Christian church. In the first centuries of the church, the debates about the sense in which Jesus was divine were fierce and brought to unsteady resolution in creeds long before much was said about the Spirit at all. You remember in the Apostles' Creed, God the Father is declared to be the Almighty Creator of heaven and earth, and a whole paragraph is devoted to Jesus's conception, birth, death, and resurrection. Then in the last paragraph the Holy Spirit is mentioned without definition in a list that includes also "the holy catholic church, the communion of saints, the forgiveness of sins, the resurrection of the body, and the life everlasting." Later, in the Middle Ages, the Eastern Orthodox and Roman Catholic Churches separated over a dispute as to whether the Holy Spirit proceeds from the Father alone or from the Father and Son together. This was not an edifying dispute, and theology of the Holy Spirit has more or less languished ever since.

The Holy Spirit has played a somewhat larger role in the piety of the Eastern Orthodox Churches than in Western Roman Catholicism and mainline Protestantism. The reason for this has been the Eastern emphasis on sanctification, which those churches call "theosis," or becoming more God-like. The Holy Spirit is the source of sanctification. John Wesley, the founder of Methodism, picked up the emphasis on sanctification, and with it the importance of the Holy Spirit. This distanced him from the mainline Lutherans and Calvinists who emphasized the acts of Jesus Christ in the past and in eternity, but without much enthusiasm for the freedom of the Holy Spirit in the present. Because the Holy Spirit reinterprets the Bible in the present for new occasions, the Wesleyan emphasis distances that movement from the literalist fundamentalists as well. The Wesleyan movement and its influences includes the Nazarenes, Pentecostals, and Charismatics as well as most African American religious sensibilities that emphasize the movement of the Spirit. Poor people with little investment in established institutions, and uneducated people who have no formal liturgies or biblical learning, are rightly drawn to religious practice that emphasizes the Spirit's present reinterpretation of things, making all things new. Those who have little to lose are especially responsive to the Spirit, which is often resisted by people grounded in the past.

You can see why the Holy Spirit is vaguely threatening to established churches. As new wine does not fit into old wineskins without bursting them, a Spirit-filled people does not fit into old forms without relativizing them. When new circumstances seem to be ill served by the old church structures, by the old liturgies, by the old theological expressions, by the old interpretations of the Bible and of the mind of Christ, people trusting in the Spirit are willing to try new ways.

Of course, the discernment of spirits is difficult and never infallible. To distinguish the Holy Spirit from the spirits of ambition, power, greed, lust, and nostalgia is not easy. For this reason a critical connection with the past is always necessary. Spiritual judgment about contemporary innovations should always be guided by analogy to the innovations of the past that proved to lead to the Spirit's marks of justice, joy, love, mercy, and peace. Yet think how drastic some of those past innovations have been! Think, for instance, of the invention of the Christian movement out of the Judaisms of Jesus's time, as recorded in Acts. We need to be ready in our time for drastic innovations in the evolution of Christianity.

Mark just how the Holy Spirit is dangerous, however. Permit me a moment of metaphysics, if you will, while I say what I think all those symbols of the Holy Spirit are getting at. John says that Jesus is the incarnation in human form of the Logos, the structures of things, or that which makes things harmonize into structures. The Spirit is the creativity of God within the world that builds up those structures. The creativity of God also destroys structures to build others. As you have heard me say many times, the immensity of God's creativity that builds up and then destroys to build more is wild. The Big Bang and the rush of cosmic gasses to form suns, which in turn flame out as supernovas, have no regard to the human scale of things. The fragile structure of the human habitat is a wonder of creativity, and it is subject to the other forces of creativity that will destroy it one day. The wild God is fecund beyond measure, and the manifestations of the Spirit's creativity in human experience are also wild. Any settled human structure is in danger from the wild Holy Spirit. The Spirit makes churchmen and churchwomen nervous! You can see why Paul was so nervous, in our text, to insist that the Spirit is one, when all those manifestations—wisdom, knowledge, faith, gifts of healing, miracle working, prophesy, discernment of spirits, speaking in tongues, and the interpretation of tongues—seem to be going off in different competing but compelling directions.

The Spirit of God's creativity means something a bit different on the human scale from what it means on the cosmic scale. Although human beings are free to ignore or reject the point, we live in a world surrounded by obligations to do better rather than worse. Our habits and institutions should embody those virtues I mentioned earlier: justice, joy, love, mercy, peace, and many others. Our sanctification depends on embodying them in ourselves, so that they add up to divine creativity on a human scale. The Holy Spirit comes to us as the creativity always to do better than we do now. Come to us, the Holy Spirit also is the creativity to deconstruct, destroy, and give up those things that hold us back. Sometimes this is extremely painful, especially when we remember what a glory it was to achieve in the first place those things that now hold us back. The Holy Spirit makes Christ present to us as judge. Destruction of those we love is incomprehensible to us, even when it makes room for others: such suffering and grief are in themselves gifts of the Holy Spirit, ambivalent as that is to human judgment.

With danger signs all about, the message of Pentecost, nevertheless, is to live dangerously. With all due care to test the spirits, we are urged to trust the Spirit in its creative urgings. When our community's hidebound structures entrench poverty and injustice, let us call for the Spirit to give us new directions and a new energy; let it destroy our fears and investments that reinforce evils. When our family relations and friendships feed on domination and unwarranted dependencies, let us call in the Spirit to destroy those bad ties and lead us into freer loving relations. When our personal prospects seem blocked or confused, let us call down the Spirit to show us how to possess more aptly the mind of Christ, and how to dispossess ourselves of the expectations that lead nowhere. When our souls are mired in sin, panic, and self-hate, let us call up from their depths the Holy Spirit that can create in us clean hearts and destroy the things that bind us.

Some Christians believe that what counts is what God did in the past with Jesus. I say that does *not* count *unless* the Holy Spirit can make that happen today with us. God's creative transformation is not less powerful today than in Jesus's time, and our spiritual practice gives us the teaching and example of Jesus to discern the true spirit of creative transformation. We might think we languish with a society where nothing can be done about injustice, with personal relations that starve as well as feed, with personal stories that are dead ends, with souls we would deny, even with a religion of the past that is nostalgic at best and boring at worst. But that is illusion. The Holy Spirit of God's creative love, which began the cosmos with a mighty blast and turns swarms of cosmic gasses into garden worlds like ours, pours through our lives like a mighty river surging through underground caves to burst forth in fountains of transformation. Come Holy Spirit and lead us to the crosses that destroy our evil and bondage! Come Holy Spirit and raise us to new lives in which our own creative efforts are more like God's own! Come Holy Spirit and groan in us a new and true prayer that our lives together host the God who would live incarnate among us. Amen.

34

Something New and Lasting[1]

Psalm 149; Song of Solomon 8:1–7

Marriage in our time isn't what it used to be! I bet you think I am referring to the innovation of same-sex marriage; but I'm not. Marriage in the Judeo-Christian cultures used to be a financially oriented social arrangement by which a wife was bought for a dowry price to be owned by her husband for the purpose of bearing children and managing a household. Marriage was the social form by which the fortunes of two or more families could be combined and the inheritance passed on legally from generation to generation. (In my case, my wife and I combined our college debts!) The biblical family values were that a man should take as many wives as he could afford; the custom is still followed in some Arabic Islamic cultures.

Sex was most important in marriage for the bearing of children, and barrenness on the wife's part was grounds for divorce. Because feelings of love are intimately related to sex, sometimes a marriage would blossom into a loving companionship. But love was not expected. The ideal for marriage was the mutual respect that one could hope would come from a productive, well-run household and family. Proverbs chapter 31 famously puts the expression of respect this way:

> A capable wife who can find?
> She is far more precious than jewels.

---

1. Preached June 18, 2005, in Marsh Chapel as part of the wedding of James Olson and Darrick Jackson.

> The heart of her husband trusts in her, and he will have no lack of gain.
> She does him good, and not harm, all the days of her life.
> She seeks wool and flax, and works with willing hands.
> She is like the ships of the merchant, she brings her food from far away.
> She rises while it is still night and provides food for her household,
> And tasks for her servant-girls.
> She considers a field and buys it;
> With the fruit of her hand she plants a vineyard.
> She girds herself with strength, and makes her arms strong.
> She perceives that her merchandise is profitable.
> Her lamp does not go out at night.
> She puts her hands to the distaff, and her hands hold the spindle.
> She opens her hand to the poor, and reaches out her hands to the needy.
> She is not afraid for her household when it snows,
> For all her household are clothed in crimson.
> She makes herself covering; her clothing is fine linen and purple.
> Her husband is known in the city gates,
> Taking his seat among the elders of the land.
> She makes linen garments and sells them;
> She supplies the merchant with sashes.
> Strength and dignity are her clothing, and she laughs at the time to come.
> She opens her mouth with wisdom
> And the teaching of kindness is on her tongue.
> She looks well to the ways of her household,
> And does not eat the bread of idleness.
> Her children rise up and call her happy;
> Her husband too, and he praises her.
> "Many women have done excellently, but you surpass them all."
> Charm is deceitful, and beauty is vain,
> But a woman who fears the LORD is to be praised.
> Give her a share in the fruit of her hands,
> And let her works praise her in the city gates.

That is the biblical vision of marital success and respect. Ancient marriage structures densely define the wife in these economic, management, and reproductive roles and barely define the husband at all, even as provider, except as being bound not to approach other men's women. As I say, there was no special expectation of love in the old ways of marriage.

Perhaps this is why Jesus took such a dim view of marriage and kinship family, using its metaphors for his voluntary association of those who love God as Father, but saying that he came not to bring peace but a sword among family members. I trust you will all come back for the service here tomorrow morning when I preach on that passage from Matthew in conjunction with the story of Abraham's family with his wives Hagar and Sarah, and their sons respectively, Ishmael and Isaac. You will recall that Sarah insisted that Abraham throw Hagar and Ishmael out because Ishmael liked to play with his younger brother Isaac, just about the only expression of love in the whole Abrahamic saga.

Marriage in our time isn't what it used to be, thank God! For a variety of reasons, marriage has come to be our culture's principal, though by no means only, social institution for the expression of love. Love is intimately bound up with sex, but extends far beyond that. Love develops through time as people grow, changing their identities in relation to one another. Love grows through shifts in careers and the jolts of haphazard circumstances. Love grows through the acquisition of new family members and friends. Love is never easy, because the initial attractions of sexual love get complicated very quickly. But love is the virtue most important to develop according to every religion I know. To become a full person is to become a perfected lover. Sanctification is perfection in love. For Jesus, the venue for perfecting love was the companionship of his small group of disciples. For many within the major religions, the venue for love was monastic life. But for our culture, the principal venue for perfecting love, for becoming a full person, for growing in sanctification before God, is marriage.

How wise it is, therefore, for the Massachusetts Supreme Judicial Council to insist that marriage must be open to people of the same sex! No reason whatsoever exists that would justify denying people the right to marry whose loving feelings draw them to people of their own gender. There is no legal, economic, or familial obligation that cannot be carried out by same-sex married couples. And in our time the right to pursue the deeply human sanctification of love requires openness to the lifetime commitments of marriage. If marriage were only the economic and reproductive arrangement of the ancient world, this would not be so, because that kind of marriage was not particularly good for love. For us, marriage is the main venue for maturing love and needs to be fostered for all people who are called by God to love, regardless of their sexual orientation. For religions to fail to support same-sex marriage is for them to betray the value they find in love as the way to live before the Ultimate.

All this having been preached as the Word of God for our time, there still are some weird, not to say queer, things about this marriage of Darrick and Jim. Some of these weirdnesses are incomprehensible. For instance, why the both of them should voluntarily choose to be bald is beyond all canons of reason. Yet they egg each other on in this madness. And I shall not pursue the image of the egg any farther.

Other weird things are very comprehensible. For instance, their love for each other is weird because it is not measured out like an ancient marriage contract. It knows no measure. They are like the lovers in the Song of Solomon, which had nothing to do with marriage and everything to do with love. One says to the other,

> Set me as a seal upon your heart, as a seal upon your arm;
> For love is strong as death, passion fierce as the grave.
> Its flashes are flashes of fire, a raging flame.
> Many waters cannot quench love, neither can floods drown it.
> If one offered for love all the wealth of his house, it would be utterly scorned.

Solomon's text says that such love would scorn the wealth of domesticity for which ancient marriage was praised in Proverbs. The weird genius of Jim and Darrick is that they are bringing this ancient Solomonic love to the marriage-form of our time. By wedding them we seal their love upon their hearts with a strength greater than floods and fires, death and the grave. This marriage draws down love's power that is victorious over all that might separate them from the love of God.

To be sure, let us hope that they can cook, clothe themselves, make a living, and contribute to the community as a couple. Let us pray most earnestly, however, that they might live through a long marriage in which they perfect one another in love, sealed by us here. Let us commit ourselves as their community of witnesses to defend and support them when the ways of same-sex marriage are difficult, when human misfortune and illness beset them, and when their relationship weirdly might be threatened by improved hair styles. Amen.

35

The Ambivalence of Family, or The Lesson of Hagar[1]

Genesis 21:1–21; Romans 6:1b–11; Matthew 10:21–39

What a pleasure it is to welcome all the fathers this morning, on Father's Day, especially since I am a father myself, in fact a grandfather for two months as of today! I salute my son-in-law, Jeff, the father of my granddaughter, Gwendolyn, and also my other son-in-law, Stephen, who is about to become a father in six weeks or so, God willing. Today I also think about my own father, Richard, whom I remember with ever increasing respect and love, despite the fact he died more than thirty years ago. The contours of families can be traced through the lines of fathering. Of course they can be traced just as well through the lines of mothering but this is Father's Day, and the mothers had their turn several weeks ago.

These sweet sentiments are strangely out of place, I must say, in the Revised Common Lectionary that has given us the readings for this morning. In the gospel, we have one of Jesus's more vituperative attacks on the family, saying, "Do not think that I have come to bring peace to the earth; I have not come to bring peace, but a sword. For I have come to set a man against his father, and a daughter against her mother," and so on. I'll come back to this. But first we need to conjure with the story of Abraham and Hagar.

---

[1]. Preached June 19, 2005, celebrating Father's Day.

Now, Abraham was a great hero of Israelite history. He brought his family out of Mesopotamia into Canaan and established the nation of Israel, which is named after his grandson. Both Jews and Christians look upon Abraham as the founder of their faith. The Arabs trace their ancestry to Abraham's son Ishmael, and Islam, Judaism, and Christianity are often called the Abrahamic faiths. Yet if we look at Abraham as a family man, there is much to worry about.

Abraham was a kind of nomadic war chief who traveled with a very extensive kinship family—we know most about his nephew Lot, formerly of Sodom—all of whom had many retainers, slaves, and herds; Genesis 13 says he was also rich in silver and gold. As Abraham traveled through Canaan, his forces sometimes had pitched battles with the armies of the city-states there. His wife Sarah was very beautiful in her youth, and when they visited Egypt the pharaoh was smitten with her. Not wanting to get into trouble himself, Abraham said Sarah was his sister, and the pharaoh married her. But God, in a rare moment of swift justice for adultery, even though poor Pharaoh did not know he was committing adultery, sent plagues on the Egyptians. Pharaoh found out the cause, that Sarah was Abraham's wife, and expelled Abraham's whole clan from Egypt, blaming Abraham for not being honest to claim his wife. Abraham was not the kind of man to stick up for his wife. Nor was there any suggestion that he loved her.

He seemed, however, to be obsessed with having children, and interpreted his wanderings as a journey to a land God promised to him and his descendants, who would be as numerous as the stars of the night sky. But as he and Sarah got older, they were still childless, and Abraham complained to God that the heir of his house was a Syrian named Eliezer of Damascus. (I'm not sure why Lot was not an acceptable heir within the family.) Sarah was worried about Abraham's obsession and finally told him to take her Egyptian maid, Hagar, as a wife whose child would be Abraham's family heir. Polygamy was the standard form of marriage in the biblical view for those rich enough to afford it. When Hagar became pregnant, she looked with contempt on old, barren Sarah, which was a great mistake. Sarah complained to Abraham, and Abraham said she could do whatever she wanted with Hagar. Sarah beat her, and Hagar ran away. God's angel appeared to Hagar, struggling pregnant and thirsty through the wilderness, and told her to go back to Abraham's encampment, which she did. She gave birth to Ishmael and Abraham did raise him as his heir. But then thirteen years

The Ambivalence of Family, or The Lesson of Hagar

later, Sarah in her very old age became pregnant and bore Isaac. This is where our Genesis text comes in.

Ishmael liked to play with his little brother, according to the text, and I think this is the only expression of love in the whole Abrahamic story except for the mention that Abraham loved Isaac when he agreed to murder him and offer him as a sacrifice as he thought God had commanded. Sarah's reaction to Ishmael's affection for Isaac was to have a fit of jealousy and demand that Ishmael and his mother Hagar be turned out into the desert. Of course she wanted her own son Isaac to be Abraham's principal heir rather than Ishmael, who had already been acknowledged at her own suggestion. So Abraham, who had given his senior wife to Pharaoh, gave his junior wife and her son, his heir, to death in the desert. As our text recounts, God rescued them. The Islamic version of the story is that Ishmael remained Abraham's heir, and Isaac turned out to be only a younger brother.

Now this is not an uplifting story for Father's Day. Fathers are not all perfect, as we know. But who would want a father who sent his wife to the bed of another man in order to feel safe himself? Who would want a father who was ready to kill his child because he thought God wanted that? Who would want a father who would let a senior wife disown and imperil a junior wife and her son who is the firstborn heir? The text says that Abraham was coached in most of these things by God, but we wonder who was doing the reporting.

If we look at Abraham's story, not in the context of the biblical saga of creating the Jewish and Christian peoples, but in the context of what it says about fathering, two important points stand out. First, *our* ideals for fatherhood, which derive from the ethic of Jesus and have to do with loving, teaching, and caregiving, are a far cry from the behavior of Abraham the patriarch. We should take care not to let Abraham's model, or that of a good many of the other heroes of the Hebrew Bible, influence our ideas of fatherhood too much. We can accept Saint Paul's praise of Abraham as a man of faith who followed God blindly, even to the point of readiness to kill his own son. But we should bite our tongue if there ever is a suggestion that we should behave that way ourselves, those of us who are fathers or potential ones. I suspect mothers ought not look to Sarah as a model either. The heroes and heroines of the Hebrew Bible are not good models of parenting. Although we can derive ideals for families from the larger values of the Bible, such as love, care, and responsibility, we cannot derive them from biblical models, and need to be very careful to reject the main part of biblical family values. I'll come back to this later.

Second, we need to be cautious about accepting Jesus's admonition to think of God as our Father. To be sure, to think of God as a Father rather than a warrior is an advance toward the Christian ethic of love. But we need to be discriminating about the senses in which God should be thought of as a father. In Jesus's teachings, God was like a father in being a loving caregiver, providing his children fish, not snakes, bread, not stones, and noting the fall of every sparrow. But would Jesus have thought of God as fatherly when he wiped out all humanity except Noah and his family in the flood, and nearly all the animals as well? Was it fatherly to wipe out all the people of Sodom and Gomorrah except Lot's family? Even Abraham was against that! Was it fatherly of God to side with the Israelites, and then the Christians, against all the other peoples of the world who were equally his children? Think of the biblical stories of God demanding the slaughter of all the women and children of people's defeated by God's army! Those people were God's children too. We need to be extremely thoughtful in accepting the character of God as depicted in all the parts of the Bible as fatherly.

Or to put the point another way, we need to examine biblical history, especially its depictions of God, with a moral as well as theological point of view. For that history shows all the biases of its authors, biases we take to be morally questionable as well as theologically self-serving. The Bible is the great source of the revelation that grounds and guides the Christian religion, as well as Judaism, and to a lesser extent Islam. Yet in order to understand that revelation, we need to read the Bible with discernment, both moral and theological. For, the culture of biblical times, especially regarding family as an economic and biological unit rather than a social unit of love and care, and its acceptance of slavery, contains many things we find to be morally incompatible with a social life based on the ethical principles of Judaism and Christianity.

This brings me back to the nasty things Jesus said about the family. Jesus is never recorded to have said anything positive about the family structure as he knew it, except to apply some of its metaphors to nonkinship relations, as when he said that all people who do God's will are his brothers, sisters, and mothers, explicitly denying any special status to his own brothers, sisters, and mother. That saying is recorded in Matthew 12, Mark 3, and Luke 8, all three. Luke duplicates the same saying as in our Matthew text this morning, about setting a "man against his father, and a

The Ambivalence of Family, or The Lesson of Hagar

daughter against her mother, and a daughter-in-law against her mother-in-law; and one's foes will be members of one's own household." Jesus actually was quoting the prophet Micah chapter 7, where these lines were a complaint about the degenerate times in which Micah lived. Jesus applied the lines more generally to the family structure of the society that he knew: his own gospel was so devastating to traditional family structures that it would bring not peace, but a sword, setting family members at war with one another.

I need immediately to remind us of what Jesus's main message was, although you all know it. His message was that people should emulate God's love of all creatures, including all human beings. This has direct implications for justice, peace, poverty, and care for those who need help. The way to emulate God's love, Jesus said, is to live in communities voluntarily drawn together, like his band of disciples, where people could love one another and practice the maturing responsibilities of love. The Beatitudes in Matthew chapters 5–7 and the Farewell Discourse in John 11–17 are compact summaries of Jesus's teachings. The church from very early on has taken this ideal of voluntary communities devoted to God and God-like love as its own definition. Unlike the ancient Judaism of Jesus' own religion, which defined one as a member because of a kinship identity, being Jewish, the early Christian community was open to anyone who voluntarily joined and took on the divine role of loving, with its obligations to justice, peace, care, and personal love.

In our time we have almost completely abandoned the ancient view that the family is primarily a social arrangement for managing property and producing heirs. An economic dimension is important to family life, of course, and our laws define economic rights and responsibilities. But we reject the economic exploitation of women in the ancient family, and also the belief that children are important mainly for giving parents descendants and heirs: we think children are important for themselves. We say rather that families are the most intimate social arrangements for learning how to love, where married people grow old together through all the forms of love on life's stages, where children can learn to be loved and to love, and where extended families express the mobility of love in our society. The ancient world said a woman could be divorced for being barren or an economic bad deal; Jesus was dead set against divorce in this sense, as are most of us. We regard divorce as a tragedy, but allow that its main justification is some kind of breakdown in love, however complicated this might be. That we have no-fault divorce and laws to protect children against bad parenting indicates that even family membership has a voluntary dimension, and that its highest rules have to do with good care. Our own time is not in all respects an improvement on biblical times. But in matters of family values, we have taken on Jesus's larger value of love in community, and that is an advance.

So with regard to Father's Day, we celebrate the Christian model of fatherhood as devotion to a loving community, practicing and teaching justice and peace; caring for the poor and the needy; practicing and teaching love to all family members, especially children; inspiring the love of God; and nurturing appreciation of the good, the true, and the beautiful. Parenting is much more shared these days than in the past. Many fathers are the chief economic providers for families, but many others take care of children while others earn the living. Fathers often share both economic and domestic work. There are single fathers who bear both burdens. There are fathers separated from children by divorce or the distance of independent careers, fathers who are widowed or bereft of children through death. There are new fathers with small children, and there are grandfathers of multigenerational families. Let us celebrate today with all fathers who, in any of these conditions, can bear themselves as lovers of God and love as God loves, with justice, peace, care, responsibility, and intimacy of affection. Amen.

www.ingramcontent.com/pod-product-compliance
Lightning Source LLC
Chambersburg PA
CBHW020849160426
43192CB00007B/840